FEAR NOT SHAKESPEARE'S TRAGEDIES

A Comprehensive Introduction

༄༅

Jenny Farrell

Nuascéalta

Fear Not Shakespeare's Tragedies © Jenny Farrell, 2016.

First published in Germany: *Shakespeares Tragödien–Eine Einführung,* Neue Impulse Verlag, 2016.

All rights reserved.

No part of this book may be reproduced in any form or by any means including electronic or mechanical photography, filming, recording or by any information storage and retrieval or video systems without prior permission from the publishers, Nuascéalta Teoranta.

www.nuascealta.com • info@nuascealta.com
Cover illustration and Design: © Karen Dietrich, 2016.
Interior illustrations: © Karen Dietrich, 2016.
Typesetting: Nuascéalta Teoranta.

ISBN-13: 978-1536953619

ISBN-10: 153695361X

DEDICATION

I am deeply indebted to three people in particular who instilled in me and nurtured my love of Shakespeare:

First, my father, Jack Mitchell, with whom I concurred at an early age that Shakespeare wrote in a world language. This was before I could understand more than just the sound of the words.

More recently I have shared this passion with Robert Weimann, who contributed greatly to my understanding of Shakespeare's times and theatre and who very generously answered my questions and gave me his time.

The encouragement to write this book and enormous help in every respect came from Thomas Metscher.

CONTENTS

Introduction	9
Chapter I The Context	12
A time of upheaval	12
The Renaissance	14
Elizabeth Tudor and England at War	19
James I	20
Renaissance Theatre	21
Shakespeare's Tragedies	25
Shakespeare's Life	27
Chapter II Hamlet	35
1. The plot	36
2. Who are the characters?	40
3. What is the play about?	58
4. The drama of it all	62
5. Close focus: The gravedigger scene	65
6. Note the language	68
7. The ending	71
8. Conclusions: What is the tragedy?	72
Chapter III Othello	77
1. The plot	77
2. Who are the characters?	82
3. What is the play about?	92
4. The drama of it all	94
5. Close focus: The power of manipulation	97
6. Note the language	101
7. The ending	104
8. Conclusions: What is the tragedy?	105

Chapter IV King Lear	109
1. The plot	110
2. Who are the characters?	113
3. What is the play about?	131
4. The drama of it all	133
5. Close focus: The Machiavellian's credo	137
6. Note the language	141
7. The ending	143
8. Conclusions: What is the tragedy?	143
Chapter V Macbeth	147
1. The plot	148
2. Who are the characters?	152
3. What is the play about?	167
4. The drama of it all	168
5. Close focus: The banquet scene	173
6. Note the language	175
7. The ending	177
8. Conclusions: What is the tragedy?	178
Conclusions	181
About the Author	184
Suggested Reading	185

*How many ages hence
Shall this our lofty scene be acted over
In states unborn and accents yet unknown!*

William Shakespeare, *Julius Caesar*, 3.1

INTRODUCTION

Shakespeare! The champion of drama and of the English language, who infuses our lives with meaning and beauty. His name is so iconic and immense that readers can be daunted and turn away from him. As a passionate Shakespeare-lover I seek to carve a little path of access into his work for the nervous, the doubting, and the plain disbelieving.

This is not a specialist or academic work: rather it is designed to achieve understanding, pleasure and indeed excitement when reading or seeing performed plays that are over four hundred years old. It is a starting-point and, it is hoped, a door into the world of Shakespeare and his tragedies, of which I have chosen the most famous and most frequently performed.

The book contains an initial Context chapter briefly outlining Shakespeare's times and the main ideas that were around then.[1] This chapter also provides information on the new phenomenon of purpose-built theatres and defines Shakespearean tragedy. It further sets out what we know about Shakespeare's life.

There follow self-contained, accessible chapters on *Hamlet*,

Othello, King Lear, and *Macbeth.* Their purpose is to give the reader a sense of the overall meaning of the play, based on a close reading of the text. Each chapter explores the characters and their actions, which leads to the play's main themes. One scene is selected in each play for special scrutiny—a scene the reader can look out for and enjoy in any particular performance or film of the play. We also explore why each play is a tragedy.

The biggest obstacle of all for a newcomer to Shakespeare is the Elizabethan English. So, what can be done? There is nothing wrong with getting to know a Shakespeare play first in its modern English version. There are editions of Shakespeare's plays that place the Elizabethan text alongside the modern text. Reading the modern text first and "getting to know the characters" and what they are up to can be very empowering. This might be compared to the experience of theatregoers in Beijing, Berlin or Beirut who watch a Shakespeare play in their own, modern language. English-speakers have the advantage that they can then compare and understand an increasing amount of the Elizabethan text and be amazed by its brilliance. In this book I use such an edition when I quote from the plays.[2]

FOOTNOTES

1 The purpose of the Context chapter is to set the general historical framework for Shakespeare's tragedies. My presentation of the Renaissance is therefore simplified and does not claim to do full justice to the complexities of this time.

2 *No Fear Shakespeare*, published by Spark Publishing, and also available for reading online.

CHAPTER I

THE CONTEXT

And new philosophy calls all in doubt
—John Donne, *An Anatomy of the World*

Too frequently, Shakespeare is lifted right out of his time and place and explained outside history. This becomes a real obstacle to understanding his work. Knowing something of the nature of Elizabethan society adds immensely to an appreciation of Shakespeare.

A TIME OF UPHEAVAL

Shakespeare lived from 1564 to 1616. This was a time of enormous upheaval, as modern capitalist society slowly grew out of medieval, feudal society, which had been in existence for about a thousand years.

Improving technology and increasing productivity meant that trade became more important, and with it money. Great advances were made in the finishing of cloth, soap-making, brewing, shipbuilding, and glass-making, creating whole new industries. These also included the production of gunpowder, sugar, paper etc. on a factory scale. As these industries required power-driven machinery, this in turn resulted in an increase in coalmining. And so a new class of craftsmen, merchants and traders arose and became ever wealthier and stronger. Over time, cities grew bigger and became centres of industry and trade. Money itself became a commodity. Shakespeare's plays *The Merchant of Venice* and *Timon of Athens* give us a good sense of this new situation.

England was the main producer of wool, and this could easily be sold to growing textile industries and turned into money. Land was increasingly used for sheep-farming to produce wool. Sheep-farming required pasture land, and so forests were cut down and large areas of land enclosed for this purpose. Sheep-farming also needed far fewer workers than crop-growing. Consequently, great numbers of peasants who had worked the land were now evicted, with nowhere to go. The scenes on the heath in *King Lear* put us right out there with the dispossessed of that time. Lear grasps the sheer nakedness of these people who had absolutely nothing; it is one of his great insights.

These dispossessed and dislocated peasants in their turn became a new class: wage workers in London and in the larger towns. This enormous transition from the medieval, feudal to the modern bourgeois world reached a peak in absolutism. The absolute monarchy became established in the sixteenth century, arising from the ruins of the feuding feudal class and creating societal unity. In absolutism, the old and the new existed side by side. A society came into being with a new and modern middle class, the new bourgeoisie. These changes were the hallmark of

Shakespeare's lifetime.

The characters in his plays who are linked to the older nobility or the court are often foolish, vain, pompous, superstitious or naïve regarding the machinations and manipulations of some of the younger generation. However, they also possess an "old-fashioned" sense of honour and values. Shakespeare saw this class as no longer fit to rule in an intelligent, honest and fair way. Examples of such characters are at the heart of the tragedies of *Hamlet*, *King Lear*, and *Macbeth*. Who, then, was to replace them? Questions of good kingship are frequently explored in Shakespeare's plays.

THE RENAISSANCE

The origin of bourgeois society lies in 14th-century Italy. This is where the three basic forms of capital develop: commercial, financial and industrial capital. The cultural and intellectual centre of this early modern age lies in the Renaissance and the Reformation. The Renaissance is generally held to span roughly the period from 1300 to 1600. Changing and new classes needed to justify leaving behind the old social hierarchies. Such justification necessarily led to a hitherto unprecedented way of understanding and explaining the world.

Above all, the new capitalist class had to justify their right to a share of wealth and power. A part of the argument was that all humans were equal, regardless of their place in inherited hierarchies, as well as the notion of a person's dignity in this world.

In this respect, the art of ancient Greece and Rome was inspirational. In the ancient sculptures humans were depicted as godlike and gods rather like humans. The rediscovery of the art of the ancients inspired the artists of this new age.

The Renaissance began in Italy, and artists such as Leonardo da Vinci and Michelangelo created in their art such a Renaissance ideal of humankind. And Leonardo himself was not only a painter but also an engineer, inventor, and scientist.

An echo of the Renaissance vision of humankind is captured in Hamlet's words,

> What a piece of work is a man! How noble in reason, how infinite in faculty! In form and moving how express and admirable! In action how like an angel, in apprehension how like a god! The beauty of the world.
>
> (*Hamlet*, 2.2.299–304)

The emphasis on the human individual brought with it a different understanding of individuality, personality, character, and the psyche. A new kind of literature blossomed, expressing this.

However, it must be noted that the reality of early modern (capitalist) society was far removed from this Renaissance ideal of humankind—as indeed Hamlet also expresses at that same point in the play. This society was characterised by wars, growing colonialism, and merciless brutality. The Renaissance image of human perfection and dignity was at that time, and continues to be to this day, an expression of human potential that reaches into a kind of society where people are not crippled in their humanity. You may call it utopian.

SCIENCE

The dawn of this modern age is also marked by the birth of modern science, which reinforced the transformation in understanding society and nature.

Nicolaus Copernicus discovered that the sun, not the earth, is at the centre of the solar system. This new, revolutionary understanding was further developed, above all by the Italian Giordano Bruno and Shakespeare's contemporary Thomas Digges, who concluded through observation and calculation that the universe is infinite.[3]

The new science was based on experiment and experience. Doubt becomes the principle of the method. Another contemporary of Shakespeare's, the philosopher and scientist Francis Bacon, is deemed the "father" of this empirical scientific method. He even developed a philosophical materialism that goes far beyond his predecessors.

Hamlet possesses such theoretical curiosity that leads to new philosophical and scientific understanding. Shakespeare's portrayal of scientifically aware characters, his dismissal of superstition as outdated, as well as his searching questioning of social order, are indications of his being completely in tune with the most forward-thinking forces of his time.

THE REFORMATION

The new social forces in Elizabethan England—even where they remain in a courtly context—also justify themselves ideologically in theology and religion. The Reformation allowed the individual believer a much greater scope in independent decision-making than the Catholic Church. The Reformers protested against clerical corruption and hypocrisy. Their reformed (Protestant) version of Christian belief advanced the idea that the believer and God could communicate directly, without the help of a clerical hierarchy.

This justification of interaction without middlemen in religion was transferred to society. In other words, the new middle class felt entitled to leave their inherited place on the social scale, explore new markets, tackle great powers, and conquer the world.

The revolutionary peasants took the idea of human equality in its radical forms far beyond that of the bourgeoisie. In time the Reformation became the vindication for peasant risings in different parts of Europe. It still provided the ideological rationale for the English Revolution of 1640–1660[4] ; and in 1649, only thirty-three years after Shakespeare's death, a king was first beheaded.

The religious conflict between Reformation and Counter-Reformation led to an atmosphere of political terror throughout Shakespeare's lifetime.

CONFLICTING POTENTIALS: HUMANISM AND MACHIAVELLIANISM

Early capitalist society was marked by an uninhibited pursuit of power on the one hand and a new, humanist image of humankind in the arts on the other. New thinking developed, which gave expression to humanism as well as to unbridled pragmatism, Machiavellianism.

Renaissance humanism was the new approach to learning in schools and universities. Humanists sought to prepare students for full participation in society, by emphasising the subjects we now call the humanities. The aim was to create a citizenry that would be informed, eloquent, and capable of political involvement. Hamlet's university of Wittenberg, in Germany, was a centre of humanism and indeed of the Reformation.

Erasmus of Rotterdam, and Thomas More in England, are examples of humanist scholars in the early sixteenth century. Both explored ways of improving society and the best kind of government. They had confidence in the new class and in the unlimited possibilities of humanity.

Erasmus wrote a treatise in 1516 on *The Education of a Christian Prince*, and Thomas More, actively involved in state politics in London, and beheaded by Henry VIII in 1535, wrote the book *Utopia*, describing a fair, equal and classless society. Erasmus expects a prince to "follow the right, do violence to no one, plunder no one, sell no public office, be corrupted by no bribes."[5] He condemns war: "War is sown from war; from the smallest comes the greatest; from one comes two; from a jesting one comes a fierce and bloody one, and the plague arising in one place, spreads to the nearest peoples and is even carried into the most distant places. A good prince should never go to war at all unless, after trying every other means, he cannot possibly avoid it. If we were of this mind, there would hardly be a war." [6]

Erasmus's book was written partly in response to the Italian Niccolò Machiavelli, who was a very well-known author at that time. In his book *The Prince* Machiavelli justifies the use of all means, including violence and murder, to achieve and maintain power, regardless of what kind. Such a prince, according to Machiavelli, is entitled to pursue his purpose without mercy: ". . . being often forced, in order to preserve his Princedom, to act in opposition to good faith, charity, humanity, and religion . . . he ought not to quit good courses if he can help it, but should know how to follow evil courses if he must."[7] Machiavelli has a cynical view of humans—"the world is made up of the vulgar"[8] —and believes that a "prince, therefore, should have no care or thought but for war."[9] This ultimately rationalises a ruler's right to hurt and harm in pursuit of power, the end justifying the means.[10]

The disappearance of old hierarchies in early capitalism made possible not only utopian thinking about a new and equal society for all, as advocated in the writings of Erasmus and other humanists. It unleashed at the same time the potential for unrestrained, extreme self-interest. Machiavelli's theory is a defining principle of Renaissance capitalism that was anything but peaceful or humane. Humanism and Machiavellianism represent the potentials inherent in Renaissance society.

The Machiavellian principle as the inhuman potential is what Shakespeare warns against in all his tragedies and one he pitches against the humane alternative of his time, humanism.

ELIZABETH TUDOR AND ENGLAND AT WAR

Shakespeare grew up under the rule of Queen Elizabeth I, the daughter of Henry VIII. She was a powerful and clever politician. Her great historic achievement was to balance the power between the nobility and the court on the one hand and the growing middle class and parliament on the other. Under her rule, England became a prosperous world power.

It is a tribute to Elizabeth I, to some degree at least, that women in Shakespeare are presented as highly intelligent people, often surpassing men in their understanding and daring, for instance Portia in *The Merchant of Venice*, Cordelia in *King Lear*, and Emilia in *Othello*. Elizabeth I was a patron of Shakespeare's theatre company and saw many of his plays.

Nevertheless there was censorship, and "mutinous" playwrights, such as Ben Jonson, were occasionally imprisoned, the innocent Thomas Kyd was tortured on the horrific rack, and Christopher Marlowe may even have been assassinated. Yet radical thinking in the theatre was practised to a greater degree in England than elsewhere in Europe.

Under Elizabeth Tudor's rule England was in a constant state of war, especially for close to twenty years with Spain, from 1585 to 1604. There was also bloody conflict with Ireland: the Desmond Rebellions spanned three decades, from the 1560s to the 1580s, and the Tyrone Rebellion (Nine Years' War) from 1594 to 1603.

Wars were an ever-present feature in Shakespeare's time—not wars at home but with other countries, or at sea. A great deal of expenditure went on financing these conflicts. Random rounding up or "musters" meant that men between the ages of sixteen and sixty, especially the poor, could be conscripted in their homes or in public places and sent to fight abroad. This affected many thousands of men, their numbers growing especially during the war with Ireland.

War is the backdrop to many of Shakespeare's plays and is a constant reality in the tragedies considered here.

JAMES I

After Elizabeth Tudor's death in 1603 her cousin Mary's son, James Stuart—James I of England (and James VI of Scotland)—acceded to the throne.

There was more rebellion following this, resulting for instance in the Gunpowder Plot of 1605, which brought with it more persecution of Catholics, more spies and torture. As under Elizabeth, men found guilty of high treason were often hanged almost to the point of death, then emasculated, disembowelled and quartered and their severed heads put on public display. (Women were burnt at the stake.)

Although Scotland and England were two sovereign states, James was king of both in a personal union. One of James's great ambitions was to unite the territories into a new "Britain." The union flag of the English St George's cross superimposed on the Scottish St Andrew's Cross was designed by James in 1606. This was the beginning of the "Union Jack." [11]

RENAISSANCE THEATRE PLAYHOUSES

The transition from feudal to modern capitalist society was also evident in the development of the theatre. Playhouses and theatre companies with resident playwrights and actors were only coming into existence in London in the late sixteenth century. They soon became a serious business.

Before this there were no theatres or dramatists in England. Travelling troupes of actors performed outdoors, in streets and markets or on wagons. Shakespeare may have been part of such a travelling theatre group for a while before he arrived in London. The tradition of popular itinerant theatre, with its clowning and dancing and its huge entertainment value, can still be felt in Shakespeare's plays.

This medieval popular theatre mingled with the morality and mystery plays that developed in the churches in the Middle Ages. Both these traditions fed into modern Elizabethan drama.

The first permanent playhouse, called "The Theatre," was built in London in 1576 by the actor and manager James Burbage. Shakespeare's troupe, the *Lord Chamberlain's Men*, later performed here, and when "The Theatre" had to be dismantled after conflict with the landlord, who owned the land but not the building, its timbers were swiftly transported to the Bankside in London and used to build the Globe theatre in 1599.

New, permanent playhouses, as opposed to the makeshift travelling theatre shows, allowed the space and time necessary for performing longer plays, plays that were greater in scope and ambition. Shakespeare's characters are imbued with complex individuality and personality: they are fully rounded Renaissance people and go far beyond the stereotypes of the old theatrical shows. At this time the playing companies were made up of men only; women's roles were acted by teenage boys.

At times, for example in *Hamlet*, Shakespeare introduces travelling troupes into his plays, where they perform and are given an important part. Clowns and fools are also "inherited" from this popular theatre, although Shakespeare changes their function as much as he changes all characters.

Importantly, in the context of *Othello* and *King Lear* in particular, the character Vice of the medieval morality plays makes a rejuvenated appearance as modern Machiavellian man (or woman). The Vice was one of the main stock figures in the morality plays, an agent of the Devil. The main character in these shows stood for the ordinary person and was often called Everyman.

Another stock character in the morality plays was Virtue, representing the side of God. Vice and Virtue usually tried to win control over Everyman's soul. Vice frequently took the audience into his confidence, speaking to them directly, revealing his evil purpose. Shakespeare makes good use of this tradition on a new level, as we shall see.

Many Elizabethans clearly loved the theatre and went to see new plays in their thousands whenever they could. The nobility and the queen supported the new enterprise. However, there was also opposition to the theatre by the civic authorities, representing the Puritan merchant middle class in London. They called for theatres to be closed as places of vulgar distraction and worse. Therefore the earliest playhouses were built outside the walls of the City of London.

Another obstacle was the fact that the theatres had to close frequently because of the plague, which broke out regularly in London. They were closed for almost two years between 1592 and 1593 and again repeatedly during the years 1603–1610. When the theatres closed, the players left London and their playhouses and went on tour.

Shakespeare was not the only dramatist in London at this time. He was part of a small group of young authors of histories, comedies, and tragedies. Not all of them had gone to university. What they had not learnt at school they acquired by reading.

THE GLOBE THEATRE

It is the Globe that is most famously associated with Shakespeare. All the tragedies considered here were written for performance at the Globe.

The Globe was more or less round—in fact polygonal, with about twenty corners—and about 30 metres in diameter. It was three storeys high, with tiered seating on each level, like most modern theatres, and could accommodate an audience of about three thousand. The more expensive tiered seating, at 2 and 3 pence each, was under a thatched roof, while the pit was in the open air, to maximise natural lighting. The pit was the earthen standing area around the stage, occupied by the "groundlings" for an affordable 1 penny per person. Nearby bear and bull-baiting[12] events had the same entrance charge.

A rectangular "apron" stage, about 13 metres wide and 8 metres deep, stood approximately 1½ metres off the ground in the centre of the arena. Built into the middle of this stage was a trapdoor through which actors could enter from below. Over some of the stage there was a false ceiling, held up by two pillars (large painted tree trunks), called the "heavens" and painted accordingly. Actors could also descend from here through a trapdoor by means of a harness of ropes.

The Globe was designed with the stage facing north, so that the players were protected from the glare of the sun, while the "heavens" provided further cover from rain and snow.

At the far end of the stage was the "tiring house." This was curtained off and allowed actors to enter the stage from either side and perhaps also from the middle. The tiring house was so named because actors changed their attire here. In it were the changing-rooms and a prop room. The prop man had a list of costumes and props needed for a given play, which character needed them, and in which scene.

Immediately above the curtained area at the back of the stage was a row of galleries containing the "lords' rooms." These were the most expensive seats, at 5 or 6 pence each. Spectators availing of these seats were closest to the actors and no doubt had the best acoustics.

The middle gallery, or balcony, was used when the play required one, such as in *Romeo and Juliet*. Musicians also played from the balcony.

Daylight being vital, performances began at two in the afternoon, with free entertainment for the audience beforehand. A flag was flown from the Globe's flagstaff, indicating what kind of a play was being shown: red for histories, white for comedies, and black for tragedies.

When the show began there was no change in lighting. The players were out on a daylight stage, with the heads of the "groundlings" just peering over the stage. There were no intervals.

Shakespeare's Globe was built from the oak timbers of the very first professional playhouse, "The Theatre", and burned to the ground on 29 June 1613. The fire was caused by sparks from a cannon, which was situated in the roof area and was shot for special effect. This first Globe was rebuilt almost immediately, and the new building is now referred to as the Second Globe.

SHAKESPEARE'S TRAGEDIES

We are here concerned with Shakespeare's tragedies. It is essential, therefore, to understand what tragedy is. Shakespeare had no doubt been introduced at school to the ideas of the ancients concerning tragedy and comedy. Aristotle's *Poetics* would surely have been a part of the curriculum.

Aristotle's requirement in a tragedy was that pity and fear caused by the downfall of the tragic hero should be evoked in the audience. However, he specifies that "pity is aroused by unmerited misfortune, fear by the misfortune of a man like ourselves." [13]

Shakespeare and his fellow-playwrights did not adhere slavishly to the ancient rules but changed them as they needed. However, this essence of Aristotle's definition can be applied. Tragedy is not simply the presentation of extreme individual suffering, leading to the death of the main character: if this character were an evil person, then his destruction would not be tragic.

Aristotle states this clearly: "Nor . . . should the downfall of the utter villain be exhibited. A plot of this kind would, doubtless, satisfy the moral sense, but it would inspire neither pity nor fear."[14] The death of Iago in *Othello* would not be tragic but rather a relief to all. Neither are the deaths of Goneril, Regan or Edmund in *King Lear* tragic. No, tragedy must destroy something positive and valuable, something profoundly humane within the tragic hero. So, for instance, Hamlet's humanism and appreciation of humankind is eradicated; Lear's insight into the suffering of his subjects and his understanding of his likeness to all living creatures is demolished; Othello's huge capacity for love is obliterated; even Macbeth's and Lady Macbeth's deeply hidden awareness of the enormity of their bloody actions is annihilated. These characters are tragic heroes because humane qualities within them, which express human potential, are destroyed.

Aristotle writes: "There remains, then, the character ... of a man who is not eminently good and just,—yet whose misfortune is brought about not by vice or depravity, but by some error or frailty."[15]

The fall of Shakespeare's tragic heroes is brought about not by "frailty" but by their times, which overwhelm them. Regardless of the play's setting, the nature of the time onstage is that of early capitalist society, the Elizabethan and Jacobean era. Great powers at large in these times threaten to deprive the tragic heroes of their inner, humane core. The tragic heroes strive to preserve this inner substance, their dignity, even at the price of their downfall. That which is instrumental in bringing about the death of the tragic hero is the Machiavellian force of the new times. The tragic heroes struggle with this force but have too few allies to succeed. However, their inherent humanity is the measure for a new and humane society.

The tragedies therefore present us with a rift between that which is and that which might be. They suggest that the times can and must be changed, that a society free of violence, wars and human misery is in tune with human needs and lies in the future.

We shall look at the specific nature of the tragedy in relation to each play. However, it is always the capacity for humanity in the tragic hero that evokes our sympathy ("pity") and a degree of grief ("fear") at the loss and destruction of this core.

SHAKESPEARE'S LIFE

In truth, very little is known about Shakespeare the man. Even the spelling of his surname is uncertain, as Will himself used different versions.

Shakespeare was baptised in Stratford-upon-Avon, Warwickshire, on Wednesday 26 April 1564 and was probably born two or three days before this. This date, however, applies to the old Julian calendar; the calendar we use now came into operation only in 1582. Under today's Gregorian calendar Shakespeare's birthday falls on 2 or 3 May 1564.

His father, John Shakespeare, was a skilled craftsman, a glover by trade. He was also involved in the wool trade and even engaged in money-lending. Given our understanding of England at this time, Shakespeare's father was one of the new middle class, one of the bourgeoisie, in his background as a skilled craftsman and his involvement with the wool trade. Stratford lay on one of the main woolpack routes between Wales and London.

John Shakespeare's middle-class status is also demonstrated by his holding of various municipal posts in Stratford, finally that of high bailiff, or mayor in today's terms. Shakespeare's mother, Mary

Arden, on the other hand, descended from an aristocratic family with a Catholic background. William was the third of eight children and the eldest son. He had four sisters and three brothers. Three of his sisters died in childhood.

Shakespeare's family was highly respected and of some local consequence. It is assumed that Shakespeare, as a son of Stratford's high bailiff, attended the local grammar school, King's New School. This school paid good wages to teachers and attracted some highly qualified humanist teachers. It is thought that two Oxford graduates, Ben Hunt and Thomas Jenkins, were employed as masters or teachers at the time William attended the grammar school.

The age for beginning grammar school in those days was seven. Only boys attended school outside of home; girls were taught at home. Prior to entering grammar school, children aged five to six were taught to read and write English in "petty" or "Dame" schools, run by educated ladies locally in their own houses. Boys attended grammar school from six in the morning until about five in the evening in the summer and from seven in the morning until four in wintertime. The school year lasted between forty and forty-four weeks, and the pupils attended school for seven or eight years. The greatest amount of teaching was dedicated to Latin language and literature. This included performing some of the ancient plays. The boys had to speak Latin to one another and were severely punished for speaking English.

Shakespeare left school at the age of fourteen. Usually pupils would have progressed to university at this age, but Shakespeare's father had run into financial difficulties, and so William's formal schooling came to an end.

The next event about which there is certainty is

Shakespeare's marriage to Anne Hathaway in late 1582, when he was eighteen. They had three children: Susanna (born 1583) and the twins Judith and Hamnet (born 1585). Hamnet died at the age of eleven in 1596.

Apart from these dates, very little is known about Shakespeare in the years between his leaving school and being recorded as a playwright in London in 1592. The years following the birth of his twins and the first mention of him in London are therefore often referred to as the "lost years." It is thought that he joined an acting troupe and toured the country with them for some time in his youth after leaving school. Such troupes often came through Stratford, and it is possible that he became a member of one of them.

When exactly Shakespeare went to London is not clear. What is clear is that by the time he is first mentioned as a playwright he must have already been living and working there for some time, fully embarked on a life of reading, writing, and theatre work. We know this because Shakespeare was attacked by the dramatist Robert Greene as an "upstart crow" in a review that has survived.

It is therefore very likely that Shakespeare spent some considerable part of his "lost years" in London, reading and educating himself further. London was a hub for booksellers, publishers, and printers. Shakespeare's Stratford peer and neighbour Richard Field, son of a tanner, had begun an apprenticeship with London printers in 1579. Through Field and others, Shakespeare would have had easy access to books and all the new ideas of the time, which are reflected in his work.

Shakespeare wrote two long narrative poems at this time and probably also a number of sonnets. Henry Wriothesley, Earl of Southampton,[16] features as the man to whom *Venus and*

Adonis as well as *The Rape of Lucrece* are dedicated. It is also likely that he is addressed in some of the sonnets. This suggests that Shakespeare had already secured aristocratic patronage, important to his survival as a writer.

Between 1594 and 1599 Shakespeare's group, the *Lord Chamberlain's Men*, were among the most popular playing companies in London. They were frequently invited to play at the royal court.

Shakespeare bought shares in the playhouse and became a partner in this acting company. This shows that theatres were seen as business investments. Shakespeare was an actor as well as a playwright in those early days. James Burbage usually played the leading role and Shakespeare a secondary part. The famous comedian of the day, Will Kempe, was also part of the company and must have added greatly to their popular appeal.

Increasingly, Shakespeare wrote plays. He was so prolific at this time that he had earned enough money by 1597 to buy a large house in Stratford, the second-best house in the town, although he did not live there permanently until the end of his life.

On behalf of his father Shakespeare also purchased a coat of arms from the royal heralds, making him a "gentleman." In Stratford he was better known as an investor than as a dramatist. He bought and hoarded malt, to the dismay of some hungry citizens. His plays were probably never performed in his home town, as its Puritan authorities opposed such entertainment.

By 1599 Shakespeare had moved from Bishopsgate in London to Bankside, where the Globe was being constructed. In the immediate neighbourhood were many inns, brothels, bear and bull-baiting pits, and not least the notorious Clink prison. It is here, in the Globe, that most of Shakespeare's mature plays were performed.

Queen Elizabeth died on 24 March 1603 and was succeeded by James I, when Shakespeare was thirty-eight. He was yet to write some of his greatest work and about this time began to concentrate even more on writing rather than playing. While *Hamlet* was probably written about 1600, during the reign of Elizabeth, it is likely that *Othello* was composed largely after her death; it was first performed in late 1604. *King Lear* (1605) and *Macbeth* (1606) were written when James I was established on the throne.

The *Lord Chamberlain's Men* changed their name to *King's Men* in 1603. They performed at King James's court eleven times between November 1604 and October 1605, suggesting a great reputation and excellence. By this time Shakespeare had moved back into the city of London.

An event that falls in this time was the Gunpowder Treason Plot, intended for 5 November 1605. Although the blowing up of the House of Lords was thwarted, it led to a widespread campaign to seek out Catholic conspirators. It is quite likely that Shakespeare knew personally some of the people implicated in the wider circle of this planned attack, including his friend and fellow-dramatist Ben Jonson and some of his mother's extended Arden family.

In 1603 and 1606 London was hit by terrible outbreaks of plague, killing tens of thousands of people and leading to the closing of the playhouses in an effort to halt the spreading of the disease.

From 1608 the *King's Men* also performed at the indoor Blackfriars Theatre in London. This had been built by Burbage in 1596. Unlike the public Globe Theatre, it was a private theatre, catering for London's well-to-do. The charge for admission was up to five times that of the Globe, and it was equipped with a roof, artificial lighting, and other amenities not found in public playhouses.

Some time about 1611 Shakespeare returned to Stratford, where his wife and two married daughters lived. Here he composed some final plays. He died on 3 May 1616. In 1623 two of his former colleagues in the *King's Men*, Henry Condell and John Heminge, collected thirty-six of his plays and published them in a volume now known as the First Folio, along with a eulogy by Ben Jonson, in which he addresses Shakespeare as Soule of the Age!

FOOTNOTES

3 Giordano Bruno was burnt at the stake in Rome in 1600 for heresy. He had concluded that, given an infinite universe, God must exist within it, not outside it.

4 This time is often referred to as the Civil War in England. I adopt the term used by Christopher Hill and other historians, as it best reflects the period's pivotal nature in the transition from feudalism to capitalism.

5 Desiderius Erasmus, *The Education of a Christian Prince*, chapter I, "The qualities, education, and significance of a Christian prince."

6 Ibid., chapter XI, "On beginning war."

7 Niccolò Machiavelli, *The Prince*, chapter XVIII, "Concerning the way in which princes should keep faith."

8 Ibid.

9 Ibid., chapter XIV, "That which concerns a prince on the subject of the art of war."

10 We are not here concerned with the historical assessment of Machiavelli. Instead, we are looking at how he was understood by the humanists in England and in Europe. They grappled with Machiavelli's vindication of the uninhibited pursuit of power, whose unleashed violence may be employed to enforce any kind of rule. Machiavelli's demand not to shirk brutality and murder was identified as Machiavellian early on, and also in England at the time of Shakespeare. Evidence for this can be found, for example, in Christopher Marlowe's *The Jew of Malta*, where "Machiavel" appears in the Prologue, commenting on ruthlessness in the play. It is in this sense that I use the term "Machiavellianism" in this book.

11 In Scotland this Union flag showed St Andrew's cross superimposed on St George's cross.

12 Chained animals had to fight against dogs or men.

13 Aristotle, *Poetics*, chapter XIII.

14 Ibid.

15 Ibid.

16 pronounced "Rizzley."

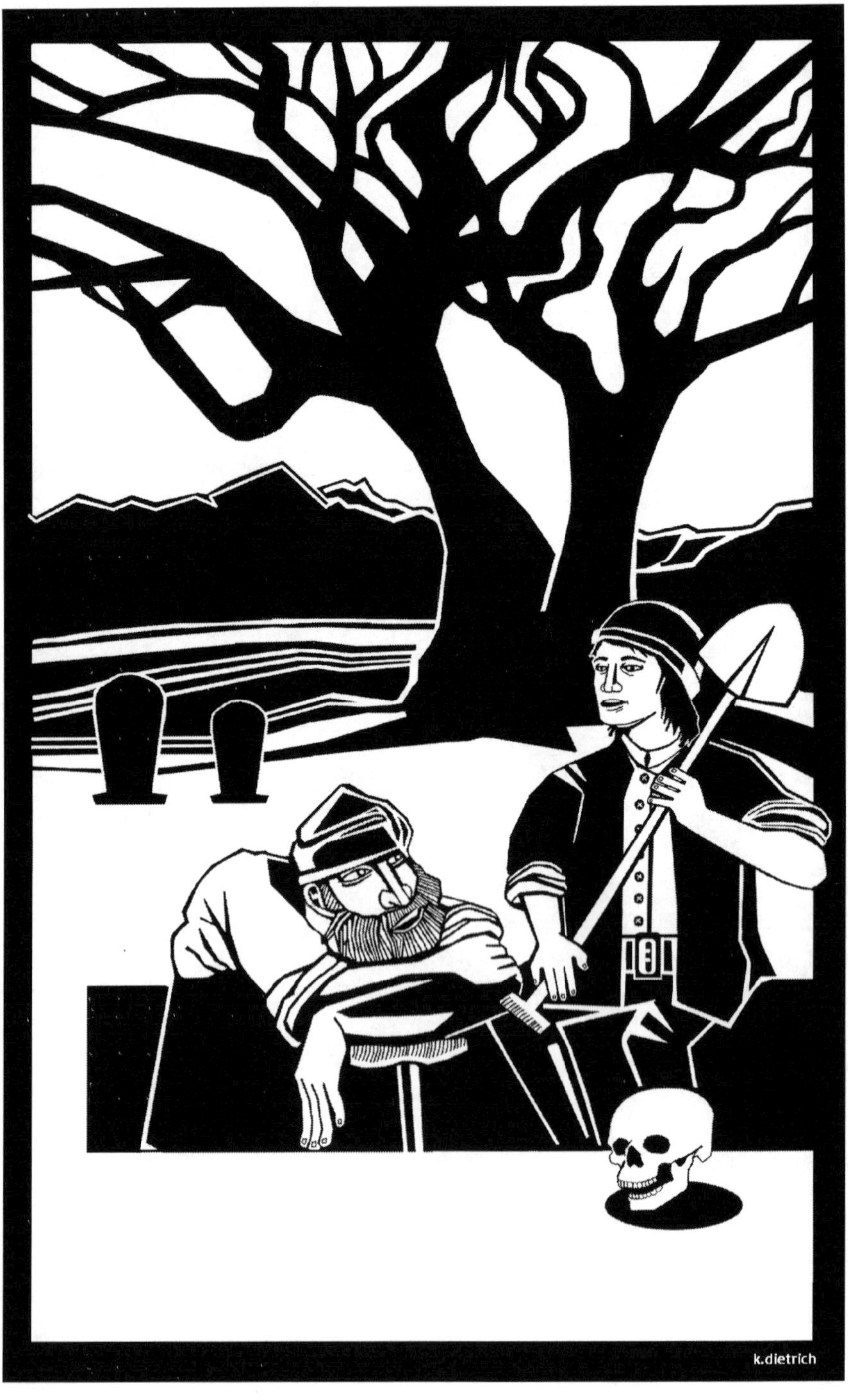
k.dietrich

CHAPTER II

HAMLET (1600)

Revenge is a kind of wild justice, which the more a man's nature runs to, the more ought law to weed it out.
—Francis Bacon, *On Revenge*

It may come as a surprise to learn that Shakespeare drew most of his material from existing sources and rarely invented a plot from beginning to end. However, what he made of the existing stories is always his very distinct and unique play. Versions of the Hamlet story were around from the twelfth century.

Hamlet comes within the genre of the revenge play, which was popular with the Elizabethans. It has roots as far back as the Roman writer Seneca, whose works were translated into English during the Renaissance.

The most obvious contemporary dramatic backdrop to *Hamlet* was Thomas Kyd's hugely successful play *The Spanish Tragedy*, which also involves a ghost, a demand for revenge, a play within a play, and madness. There was another play called

Hamlet in the 1580s, thought to have been written by Thomas Kyd. This is now lost.

Hamlet is Shakespeare's longest play, with over 4,000 lines, and a full performance takes a good four hours.

The setting for *Hamlet* is Denmark in the relatively recent past for the audience at the time. The most specific contemporary reference is the one to Wittenberg University, the sixteenth-century centre of the Reformation and a seat of humanist learning. This was Martin Luther's university and also that of the fictional Dr Faustus. Hamlet and Horatio are students at the university when the play begins.

1. THE PLOT

The play opens dramatically, with a ghost appearing before the watchmen at the Danish royal palace, just after midnight. The ghost looks like their dead king, "fair and warlike" (1.1.45). As the ghost has appeared over a number of days now, the guards have asked "a scholar" (1.1.40) to see and speak to it. Horatio, confronted with the ghost, is torn between superstition and science. He and the guards decide to tell Prince Hamlet about the ghost, and Hamlet agrees to join them for the next night's watch.

There is a serious war effort going on in Denmark—caused by the dead King Hamlet's defeat of Fortinbras, king of Norway, whom he killed in battle and whose lands he took. Now young Fortinbras is threatening to claim them back by force.

Meanwhile the dead king's brother, Claudius, has married his former sister-in-law, Hamlet's mother, Gertrude. They tell young Hamlet to forget his grieving and not to return to Wittenberg University.

Laertes, son of the Lord Chamberlain, Polonius, warns his sister, Ophelia, not to believe Hamlet's courting of her. Their father also tells Ophelia to stay away from Hamlet.

Hamlet, Horatio and the guards see the ghost again. They all take it to forebode disaster. Hamlet speaks to the ghost of his father, who confirms that he was murdered by Claudius and complains of Gertrude's shallowness. The ghost asks Hamlet twice to avenge him. Hamlet, in the enormity of the moment, vows to do so.

This meeting with the ghost reinforces Hamlet's disappointment with his mother, and confirms his suspicion regarding deceptions at court. He decides to put on an act of madness, in order to establish the truth. Act 1 ends with Hamlet declaring that this is not just a matter of revenge: there is something fundamentally wrong with the time he lives in, and he undertakes to tackle this.

When Ophelia speaks to Polonius we discover that Hamlet has already begun to act as if he is mad. Ophelia believes that his behaviour is due to her rejection of him at the behest of her father. Polonius resolves to take her to the king with this story.

In the meantime Polonius has sent Reynaldo to find out Laertes' reputation in Paris, telling him exactly how to go about spying on his son.

The king too has sent for spies, Hamlet's childhood friends Rosencrantz and Guildenstern. They are to find out what they can from Hamlet. There is a growing atmosphere of surveillance; this is compounded when Polonius suggests to Claudius that they should send Ophelia to cross Hamlet's path when he is on his own, to probe into his madness.

A troupe of players arrives to perform at the palace. Hamlet greets them and chats to them like old friends.

Following this scene Claudius and Polonius hide and listen as "lawful espials" (3.1.33) when Hamlet and Ophelia meet. In some performances of this scene Hamlet becomes aware of, or expects, this planned spying. This helps to explain why he challenges Ophelia the way he does. In Hamlet's view Ophelia is in league with Claudius. While Ophelia is taken in by his pretended madness, Claudius is not, as he comments, "Was not like madness" (3.1.164) and decides to send Hamlet "with speed to England" (3.1.169).

As the players prepare for their show Hamlet meets Horatio and tells him of his plan to use the play to establish the guilt or otherwise of Claudius. He asks Horatio to join him in observing Claudius and to compare notes after the play.

The play is preceded by a dumb show, summarising the plot of a king poisoned in his sleep and his wife marrying the poisoner. When this scene is enacted, Claudius rises, calls for a light, and leaves. All exit except Hamlet and Horatio, who agree that Claudius is guilty, as the ghost had said.

Hamlet is called to his mother's chamber. He resolves to confront her. En route he passes Claudius, apparently in prayer. Although he could kill him easily at this time, he doesn't, arguing that Claudius would then go straight to Heaven, having just cleansed his soul by prayer.

When Hamlet reaches his mother's room he mistakenly kills Polonius. Hamlet shames his mother into admitting her betrayal. The ghost enters at this point to remind him of his revenge. Hamlet makes it clear to his mother that he is not mad, and asks her not to betray him to Claudius. He also tells her that Claudius is planning to send him to England to get rid of him.

When Gertrude returns to Claudius she confirms that Hamlet is mad, as evidenced by his killing of Polonius. Claudius is now convinced he is in danger and that Hamlet must go. He sends him to England by ship, in the company of Rosencrantz and Guildenstern, carrying a letter for the King of England demanding the "present death of Hamlet" (4.3.67).

In a short but important scene Fortinbras appears on his way through Denmark to Poland to fight over a tiny, barren piece of land. Hamlet is horrified at such waste of life and, unconvincingly, resolves to avenge his father.

Meanwhile Horatio brings Ophelia before Gertrude to witness that this young woman has lost her mind from the shock of Hamlet's sudden madness and her father's demise. When Claudius comments ironically to Gertrude that the reason for Ophelia's madness is "her father slain" (4.5.77), it is clear that Gertrude does not know that Claudius killed Hamlet's father.

Laertes appears before Claudius and Gertrude, enraged and seeking revenge for his father's death. Gertrude rushes to Claudius's defence, insisting that he did not kill Polonius. Ophelia returns, and Laertes has a double reason for vengeance, as he witnesses her mental distress.

Sailors seek out Horatio and give him a letter from Hamlet. In it Hamlet tells his friend briefly of his fate since boarding the ship for England and asks him to have letters brought to the king. The king is in conversation with Laertes when he receives this notice of Hamlet's return to Denmark. Claudius craftily ensnares Laertes in a plan to kill Hamlet in a fencing match with a poisoned foil, and a poisoned drink for extra certainty.

Act 5 opens with two gravediggers digging a grave. They criticise social inequities and joke about their own importance. Basic human equality is emphasised as they discuss the nature of death with Hamlet and Horatio. It is only when Ophelia's funeral procession reaches them that Hamlet realises that Ophelia has died.

Hamlet tells Horatio about Claudius's letter to the King of England, requesting to have him put to death, and about how he escaped this but has sent Rosencrantz and Guildenstern to their deaths instead. At this point Hamlet asks Horatio if it would not now be morally defensible to kill Claudius, it now being an act of retribution rather than revenge.[17]

A messenger brings Hamlet a note from Claudius inviting him to a fencing match with Laertes. Before they fence, Hamlet asks Laertes for forgiveness and is forgiven. Both are very half-hearted about the fighting.

Claudius urges them on and prepares the poisoned wine for Hamlet. However, Gertrude drinks it instead. As she dies, so does Laertes, who discloses Claudius's murderous plan before he too, wounded by his own poisoned foil, expires. Hamlet uses the poisoned tip to wound Claudius and also forces him to drink the remains of the lethal wine.

Before Laertes and Hamlet die they fully forgive each other, and Hamlet begs Horatio to live and tell this story.

As the play closes there is the "warlike noise" (5.2.351) of Fortinbras approaching from his war in Poland. He has Hamlet's "dying voice" (5.2.358) as the new King of Denmark.

2. WHO ARE THE CHARACTERS?

HAMLET

Hamlet is introduced in scene 2 of act 1, following the highly dramatic appearance of the ghost in the opening scene. He appears at court with his mother, Gertrude, and Claudius. His tendency to speak with double meanings is evident in his first remarks. When Claudius calls him "my cousin Hamlet, and my son," he comments aside: "A little more than kin and less than kind" (1.2.64–65), winning the sympathy of the audience, saying he is more than a relative (kin) and their relationship is less than kind.[18] Upon being rebuked for grieving, being under a cloud, he says: "Not so, my lord. I am too much i' the sun" (1.2.67), punning on the word "son." He expresses more clearly to his mother his shock at the superficiality of her grieving, pouncing on her word "seems": "I have that within which passeth show" (1.2.85).

In his first soliloquy Hamlet vents genuine disgust at the speed with which his mother remarried and at "Things rank and gross in nature" (1.2.136) at the court in Denmark. This makes him feel suicidal.

Hamlet, like Horatio, is established as a scholar from the start: indeed his modern academic background is emphasised, as Gertrude and Claudius prevail on him not to return to study at Wittenberg.

Hamlet, Horatio and the guards meet to observe the ghost, and the soldiers pledge their "duty to your honour." Hamlet replies: "Your loves, as mine to you" (1.2.252–253), offering friendship and equality, rather than hierarchy, in their relationship. This too is a sign of the new times and humanist philosophy.

Hamlet believes in the validity of the ghost and its message and tells Horatio: "There are more things in heaven and earth, Horatio, | Than are dreamt of in your philosophy" (1.5.168–169). He also confides that he is going to pretend he has gone mad: "As I perchance hereafter shall think meet | To put an antic disposition on" (1.5.172–173). By putting on this act of madness

Hamlet is buying in to the rules of court, of "seeming," of putting on appearances.

Hamlet grasps that there is more at stake than simply avenging a murder. At the end of act 1 he exclaims: "The time is out of joint. O cursèd spite, | That ever I was born to set it right" (1.5.189–190). Here he expresses his understanding that there is something fundamentally wrong with his time. An unfathomable, new force has "dis-appointed" his father (1.5.77—my hyphen), i.e. removed his appointment as king. Hamlet, the Wittenberg scholar, feels he was born to tackle this. The old hierarchies and loyalties can no longer be relied upon.

Hamlet begins with his pretended madness right away.

His childhood friends Rosencrantz and Guildenstern are sent for to find out what is the matter with Hamlet. Just how Hamlet takes to all this double-dealing is evident when he appeals to Rosencrantz and Guildenstern's honesty: "Were you not sent for? ... Come, come, deal justly with me" (2.2.268–269).

A travelling troupe of players arrives. Hamlet is very much at ease with the actors and speaks to them as equals, familiar with their lives. He asks them to recite lines from a play about the destruction of Troy by the Greeks and especially about the role played in this by Pyrrhus, who slaughtered King Priam. His own familiarity with the text and the fact that senseless killing is the theme illuminate what is on his mind. He asks the actors to perform *The Murder of Gonzago* in their show before the King.

In a soliloquy Hamlet blames himself for not taking bloody revenge for his father's murder. However, he then challenges the whole concept of mindless medieval revenge: only Claudius and Gertrude's reaction to the play will prove or disprove their guilt. Hamlet shows himself to be a humanist. He needs to verify facts before rushing into revenge and murder.

When Hamlet next appears on stage he seems to be continuing these thoughts, contemplating the implications of taking action. This most famous passage from the play, and perhaps in all of Shakespeare, occurs just before he meets Ophelia in a situation contrived by Polonius for spying on him:

> To be, or not to be? That is the question—
> Whether 'tis nobler in the mind to suffer
> The slings and arrows of outrageous fortune,
> Or to take arms against a sea of troubles,
> And, by opposing, end them?
>
> (3.1.57–61)

Hamlet is asking himself whether he should take up weapons to fight wrongs or rather suffer them in the mind. He also contemplates the essence of being alive: to suffer in the mind or to act. The suggestion is that fighting ills will lead to his death. He then considers death as perhaps a happy alternative to life in what is described as an existence fraught with:

> Th' oppressor's wrong, the proud man's contumely,
> The pangs of despised love, the law's delay,
> The insolence of office
>
> (3.1.72–74)

In these images, the audience recognises its own society as well as Hamlet's experience. However, in the end he explains why he shirks taking up arms:

> Thus *conscience* does make cowards of us all,

> And thus the native hue of resolution
> Is sicklied o'er with the pale cast of thought,
> And enterprises of great pith and moment
> With this regard their currents turn awry,
> And lose the name of action.
>
> (3.1.84–89, emphasis added)

Conscience, Hamlet's inner guide to ethical behaviour, his humanist understanding of right and wrong, stands in the way of revenge.

When Hamlet enlists Horatio's help in observing Claudius, he describes Horatio as his soulmate: "Since my dear soul was mistress of her choice | ... her election | Hath sealed thee for herself" (3.2.56–58). Interestingly, he also commends him on his balance of passion and reason:

> And blessed are those
> Whose blood and judgment are so well commingled,
> ...
> Give me that man
> That is not passion's slave, and I will wear him
> In my heart's core, ay, in my heart of heart,
> As I do thee.
>
> (3.2.61–67)

Here Hamlet hints again at the importance of reason, of retribution rather than a blood-begetting cycle of passion-driven revenge.

When Hamlet is called to his mother's chamber after the chaos in which the play ended he resolves to challenge her verbally but not physically: "I will speak daggers to her but use none" (3.2.371).

Once with his mother, the hidden, spying Polonius gives himself away and Hamlet kills him, mistaking him for Claudius. But Hamlet is not very concerned about his death, seeing in Polonius the incarnation of dishonesty:

> Thou wretched, rash, intruding fool, farewell.
> I took thee for thy better. Take thy fortune.
> Thou find'st to be too busy is some danger.
>
> (3.4.32–34)

Alone with his mother, Hamlet becomes intensely emotional, chastising her for her immorality. He ends up winning her over to his side, asking her not to reveal to Claudius that he is perfectly sane.

When Hamlet is called upon by Claudius to reveal the whereabouts of Polonius's body he answers not so much like a madman but in the tradition of the truth-telling Fool, voicing a materialist view of death:

> *Hamlet:* A man may fish with the worm that hath eat of a king, and eat of the fish that hath fed of that worm.
> *Claudius:* What dost you mean by this?
> *Hamlet:* Nothing but to show you how a king may go a progress through the guts of a beggar.
>
> (4.3.28–32)

Here Hamlet says that death treats all equally, that rank becomes meaningless, and also stresses that when all is said and done, humans are humans, and status is nothing. This is a radical statement and scientific insight, possible in Shakespeare's times with its great social upheavals and questioning of God-given hierarchies.

When Hamlet comes across Fortinbras on his way to wage war in Poland over a tiny piece of land he confronts the Renaissance vision of humankind's divinity.

> Sure, he that made us with such large discourse,
> Looking before and after, gave us not
> That capability and godlike reason
> To fust in us unused.
> (4.4.35–38)

with the reality of:

> The imminent death of twenty thousand men,
> That for a fantasy and trick of fame
> Go to their graves like beds, fight for a plot
> Whereon the numbers cannot try the cause,
> Which is not tomb enough and continent
> To hide the slain?
> (4.4.59–64)

Given this abhorrence of bloodshed, it is difficult to believe Hamlet when he concludes: "Oh, from this time forth, | My thoughts be bloody, or be nothing worth" (4.4.64–65). When he returns to Denmark, avoiding his execution in England on the order of Claudius, he meets Horatio in the graveyard. In this scene Hamlet expresses more of his humanist views. It is the scene we look at in greater depth below.

It is only now that he feels it is morally justifiable to kill Claudius. He asks Horatio for his opinion:

> Does it not, think thee, stand me now upon—

> He that hath killed my king and whored my mother,
> Popped in between th' election and my hopes,
> Thrown out his angle for my proper life
> (And with such cozenage!)—is 't not perfect conscience
> To quit him with this arm? And is 't not to be damned
> To let this canker of our nature come
> In further evil?
>
> (5.2.67–74)

This is no longer simply a matter of medieval revenge: Claudius is a violation of human nature, ready to kill and usurp at will. Hamlet wants to stop him committing any more crimes.

Before they fence, Hamlet asks Laertes for forgiveness. "Give me your pardon, sir. I've done you wrong" (5.2.213). This is an admission that the "antics" didn't work, they were counterproductive and led to the death of innocents. At the same time Hamlet is also saying that his mistake of playing the rules of the court—deception—and the rules of the old order—revenge—meant he was not himself:

> ... What I have done,
> ... I here proclaim was madness.
> Was 't Hamlet wronged Laertes? Never Hamlet.
> If Hamlet from himself be ta'en away,
> And when he's not himself does wrong Laertes,
> Then Hamlet does it not. Hamlet denies it.
> Who does it, then? His madness. If't be so,
> Hamlet is of the faction that is wronged.
> His madness is poor Hamlet's enemy.
>
> (5.2.217–226)

Hamlet was indeed not himself, the humanist scholar. This conflict between Hamlet's humanist values and his attempt to set right a time with the new means of deception and medieval revenge ultimately leads to his downfall.

In this way Hamlet clears his conscience and his soul—not knowing that he is about to die. He is the only person to face the situation honestly. Laertes and Claudius have planned Hamlet's murder.

As Laertes dies he reveals Claudius's plot, and the young men forgive each other. With both Laertes and Gertrude dead, and in the certain knowledge of his own imminent death, Hamlet kills Claudius in an act of retribution. Dying, he declares his support for Fortinbras as the new king and begs Horatio to tell this story.

HORATIO

Horatio is Hamlet's fellow-student at Wittenberg. He is called upon to verify the ghost's existence, as he is regarded as a scientist: "Horatio says 'tis but our fantasy | And will not let belief take hold of him" (1.1.21–22). Confronted with the ghost, he asks, "What art thou" (1.1.44). He believes only what is there before him: "I might not this believe | Without the sensible and true avouch | Of mine own eyes" (1.1.54–56). This appearance contradicts the modern scientific teachings at Wittenberg.

It also seems clear that Horatio is not a nobleman but probably a middle-class man:

> ... Nay, do not think I flatter.
> For what advancement may I hope from thee
> That no revenue hast but thy good spirits,
> To feed and clothe thee?

Why should the poor be flattered?

(3.2.49–52)

He is also the friend Hamlet makes contact with on returning to Denmark and with whom he is completely honest.

Horatio is the man to bring Ophelia before Gertrude when she has lost her mind. He is asked to look after her.

When Hamlet agrees to the fencing match with Laertes, although he has a bad feeling about it, Horatio counsels: "If your mind dislike anything, obey it" (5.2.205).

At the end of the play Horatio is urged by Hamlet to "tell my story" (5.2.350). It is this task that could lead us to conclude that Horatio has most in common with Shakespeare and his fellow-playwrights. Some of these, for example Christopher Marlowe, had come from middle-class artisan backgrounds[19] and won a scholarship to university.

CLAUDIUS

Claudius is the modern Machiavellian schemer and deceiver.[20] He is the man who has killed his own brother in order to take the crown. He has married the anointed king's widow, Gertrude, and he does not shrink from plotting to kill Hamlet when he finds that he cannot deceive him.

Claudius acts alone. He has duped many nobles into believing in him.

Claudius does not seem an obviously evil character at the outset. He can take people in, and Shakespeare first lets Claudius deceive the audience. He is quite charming, seems sensible and in charge of things. This appearance is indeed a trap.

Only Hamlet's reaction to him alerts the spectators. Hamlet

does not trust Claudius, as he makes clear in his first aside. Claudius tells him that grieving for his dead father has gone on far too long, that it is "To reason most absurd" (1.2.103).

The first admission by Claudius of his villainy comes in act 3, scene 1, where he reacts to Polonius's comment: "with ... | ... pious action we do sugar o'er | The devil himself" (48–50). Claudius says in an aside, "Oh, 'tis too true! | How smart a lash that speech doth give my conscience" (3.1.50–51).

However, Claudius deceives everybody, including Gertrude, about his true character and motives, his murderous deed, and his readiness for further killing. Yet he is clearly startled when the mousetrap play presents him with his own crime.

A more explicit admission of his guilt comes with his attempt at prayer in act 3, scene 3:

> Oh, my offence is rank. It smells to heaven.
> It hath the primal eldest curse upon't,
> A brother's murder. Pray can I not.
>
> (37–39)

In a moment of honesty that anticipates Macbeth's early anxieties, Claudius, as he attempts to pray, knows he cannot expect God's forgiveness for murder if he continues to hold on to the gains, "My crown, mine own ambition, and my queen" (3.3.56). And he has no intention of giving these up.

Claudius is one of the few characters in the play who do not believe in Hamlet's assumed madness. He understands that Polonius was killed in his stead and plans to get rid of Hamlet as a matter of urgency.

Claudius very cleverly manipulates Laertes' rage to use him to kill Hamlet. Ironically, both Claudius and Laertes disregard aspects that got in the way of Hamlet's revenge: Claudius supports Laertes' idea that Hamlet might be killed in a church, and he warns him not to change his mind about avenging his father and sister.

GERTRUDE

Gertrude is introduced as a woman who echoes the sentiments of her new husband. However, she suspects that the reason for Hamlet's "madness" lies in "His father's death and our o'erhasty marriage" (2.2.57). This is honest, at least.

She is further shown to comply with Claudius's wishes and those of Polonius in agreeing to employ Rosencrantz and Guildenstern as informers on Hamlet. She is aware that Ophelia will be used to facilitate further observation, and also acquiesces in being exploited in a similar way herself: to speak to Hamlet after the play, in pretended privacy, with Polonius listening. However, after Polonius is killed in his hiding-place by Hamlet she is truly alone with Hamlet. He entreats her to really look at herself and her actions, and she responds:

> O Hamlet, speak no more!
> Thou turn'st mine eyes into my very soul,
> And there I see such black and grainèd spots[21]
> As will not leave their tinct.
>
> (3.4.89–92)

She is kind to Ophelia and genuinely regrets her death. However, she seems to drift back towards Claudius's deceptions later on in the play. She is clearly unaware of his plan to eliminate Hamlet and therefore unwittingly drinks the poisoned wine designed for her son.

POLONIUS

Polonius is the Lord Chamberlain, and the father of Laertes and Ophelia. He is the most important man at court after the king and queen. He is the king's loyal servant, no matter who the king is.

He is aware of the affairs at court and instructs Laertes in the ways of the world and how best to get on in it. Among these tips is that he should not say what he thinks: "Give thy thoughts no tongue," "Give every man thy ear but few thy voice" (1.3.59, 68), Polonius's own maxim.

He is an expert in surveillance. He has no scruples about sending a spy after his son. He also suggests to Claudius that Ophelia might be used as a tool to get to the root of Hamlet's madness, which he fondly believes to be Hamlet's love for Ophelia.

Moreover, it is Polonius's idea to use Gertrude to extract confidences from Hamlet, with himself as spy:

> ... after the play
> Let his queen mother all alone entreat him
> To show his grief. Let her be round with him,
> And I'll be placed, so please you, in the ear
> Of all their conference.
> (3.1.181–185)

This proves to be his undoing, and only his children grieve for him.

OPHELIA

Ophelia has received Hamlet's attentions since he returned to the court. Both her brother and her father warn her and tell her that these attentions are false. Ophelia is clearly uncertain of herself and has been brought up to obey her father, and so this conditioning determines her behaviour: "I shall obey, my lord" (1.3.136).

In act 2, scene 1 she is the first to report Hamlet's "antic" behaviour, which she believes is due to her having refused his letters and visits, resulting in madness. She consents to Polonius's plan to inform on Hamlet by letting the conversation between them be overheard, thereby becoming part of the web of deceit. Her allegiance at this point is with her father and her king—a betrayal of Hamlet that he considers unforgivable. Hamlet's touchstone is honesty and loyalty. As he feels this is not forthcoming from Ophelia, he treats her harshly and crudely, both in the scene contrived by Polonius and when they sit side by side to watch the players perform *The Murder of Gonzalo*.

His main point regards Ophelia's honesty. Honesty is Hamlet's measure when it comes to judgement of character. He sees Ophelia, like Rosencrantz and Guildenstern, involved with the intrigues at court and as disloyal to him.

The next time Ophelia appears she has become genuinely mad, with the grief over the loss of Hamlet and her father's death. Although Ophelia's madness is not contrived, she too expresses truths that are deeply felt. She doesn't use clever wordplay for this but songs, snatches of folk tales, and the language of flowers. She gives wild flowers to the people around her that have specific connotations:

> There's fennel[22] for you, and columbines.[23]—There's rue[24] for you, and here's some for me. We may call it

"herb of grace" o' Sundays.—Oh, you must wear your rue with a difference.—There's a daisy.[25] I would give you some violets,[26] but they withered all when my father died.

(4.5.179–183)

Ophelia continues to "speak" in the language of flowers when she dies in the river:

There with fantastic garlands did she come
Of crowflowers,[27] nettles,[28] daisies,[29] and long purples,[30]
That liberal shepherds give a grosser name,
But our cold maids do "dead men's fingers" call them.

(4.7.167–170)

The stream where Ophelia's life finds an end is fittingly overhung by a weeping willow.

LAERTES

Laertes travelled to Denmark from Paris for the new king's wedding. He warns Ophelia that a royal will not marry below his rank. With these words he expresses his own views of deceptions and betrayal at court.

Laertes returns again from Paris when he hears of Polonius's death. He is intent on revenge. In this way he is a foil to Hamlet. Laertes has no second thoughts or misgivings. He is ready to kill Hamlet, no matter how or when, and doubly so after he witnesses Ophelia's insanity.

Laertes, like Hamlet, is loved by the people, and we hear the people of Denmark calling for Laertes to be made king. Yet he does not convince the audience that he is fit to be king. He has neither principles nor real understanding. He is taken in by Claudius, who uses him as a puppet.

When Hamlet apologises for the wrongs he has inflicted, Laertes is tellingly torn between his instinct and his "honour":

> ... I am satisfied in nature,
> Whose motive in this case should stir me most
> To my revenge. But in my terms of honour
> I stand aloof, and will no reconcilement
> Till by some elder masters, of known honour,
> I have a voice and precedent of peace
> To keep my name ungored.
>
> (5.2.231–237)

At this point Claudius could be that "elder master" who might "keep" Laertes' "name ungored." But of course he will not. Even in the middle of the fencing match Laertes comments that "it is almost 'gainst my conscience"[31] (5.2.298). And it is Laertes who, dying, uncovers the plot and tells Hamlet, "The king, the king's to blame" (5.2.322).

FORTINBRAS

Fortinbras is the old King of Norway's son. He threatens to claim lost Norwegian territories back by force, and he has gathered an army of mercenaries to do so: "Sharked up a list of lawless resolutes, | For food and diet" (1.1.97–98).

In some ways Fortinbras, like Laertes, is a foil for Hamlet. However, Fortinbras expresses no desire to avenge his father, slain by Hamlet's father: all he wants is to retrieve forfeited lands.

Claudius sends messengers to the bedridden King of Norway to dissuade his nephew, young Fortinbras, from taking back his territories. The uncle recalls Fortinbras and tells him to invade Poland instead, begging of Claudius free passage through Denmark.

Fortinbras's purpose is pointless warfare. He is willing to sacrifice the lives of twenty thousand men for no reason.

On the other hand, what you see is what you get. There is no double-dealing about Fortinbras. Perhaps this is why Hamlet votes for him as king as he dies. While Fortinbras represents the old order, doomed to pass into history, he is acceptable for a short while.

OLD KING HAMLET

We encounter Old King Hamlet only as his ghost.[32] The ghost sets Hamlet the task of avenging his death. He thereby evokes the old medieval code of honour.

> Interestingly, the ghost regrets that he was
> Cut off even in the blossoms of my sin
> . . .
> No reckoning made, but sent to my account
> With all my imperfections on my head.
>
> (1.5.76–79)

In other words, he was murdered without receiving absolution. He also tells Hamlet not to burden his mind or soul with taking revenge on his mother. Instead he hopes for God to punish her:

> But howsoever thou pursuest this act,
> Taint not thy mind, nor let thy soul contrive
> Against thy mother aught. Leave her to heaven
> And to those thorns that in her bosom lodge
> To prick and sting her.
>
> (1.5.84–88)

Some comic relief is provided by the ghost demanding oaths of secrecy from the watchmen, calling up from underneath the stage.

The ghost appears to Hamlet for a second time in his mother's chamber. Gertrude cannot see or hear the ghost. It comes to remind Hamlet of his revenge—"to whet thy almost blunted purpose"—but also to ask Hamlet to treat Gertrude kindly: "O, step between her and her fighting soul" (3.4.112–114).

ROSENCRANTZ AND GUILDENSTERN

Rosencrantz and Guildenstern are Hamlet's friends. They are comic in that they have no individuality. Hamlet speaks to them in prose from the start, not in verse, as would be fitting for his status. He forces them to admit that they were recruited by Claudius as informers.

Increasingly, he sees them accurately as being more loyal to the king than to himself. He now really puts on antics for them, telling them truths in such a jesterly fashion that they don't understand.

Laughing at Guildenstern, who insists he cannot play the recorder, Hamlet states that he is amazed that his erstwhile friend believes he can "play" Hamlet, i.e. find out what is going on in him:

> Why, look you now, how unworthy a thing you make of me! You would play upon me. You would seem to know my

stops. You would pluck out the heart of my mystery. You would sound me from my lowest note to the top of my compass. And there is much music, excellent voice, in this little organ, yet cannot you make it speak? 'Sblood, do you think I am easier to be played on than a pipe? Call me what instrument you will, though you can fret me, yet you cannot play upon me.

(3.2.336–344)

Hamlet ultimately sends them to their deaths, by changing the letter they are carrying to the English king with an execution order for Hamlet. His justification for this echoes his earlier comment at Polonius's death:

Why, man, they did make love to this employment.
They are not near my conscience. Their defeat
Does by their own insinuation grow.
'Tis dangerous when the baser nature comes
Between the pass and fell incensèd points
Of mighty opposites.

(5.2.60–65)

He sees them as opportunists and traitors.

3. WHAT IS THE PLAY ABOUT?

THE STRUGGLE BETWEEN HUMANISM AND MACHIAVELLIANISM

This play is about the struggle to the death between humanism and Machiavellianism. Hamlet, the humanist scholar, and

Claudius, the dangerous Machiavellian, are the only two characters in the play who fully understand what is at stake. Both realise that one of them is going to die, that they are mutually exclusive.

How they face this challenge is defined by their character. Hamlet is at first urged by his father's ghost to avenge his killing. He is determined to establish Claudius's guilt and resolves on retribution only when he can document Claudius's ruthlessness. He has seen that Claudius is a "kindless villain" (2.2.558). He considers him to be without kindness, and without kind—not human.

Claudius, true to his Machiavellian nature, is clever, deceitful, and ruthless. He does all in his power to have Hamlet killed. He exploits the weaknesses of others, for instance Polonius, Gertrude, and Laertes; yet he comes up against human kindness, his anathema, time and again, which creates obstacles for him. He ends up sacrificing his wife and his own life as a penalty for his evil.

THE THEME OF WAR

Linked to this struggle between inhumane violence and human kindness is the opposition of revenge and retribution, war and peace. War is a constant presence in the play, beginning with Old Hamlet's appearance in armour, which he seems to have worn frequently during his lifetime. There is a major war effort going on in Denmark as the play opens:

> Why this same strict and most observant watch
> So nightly toils the subject of the land,
> And why such daily cast of brazen cannon

> And foreign mart for implements of war,
> Why such impress of shipwrights, whose sore task
> Does not divide the Sunday from the week.
> What might be toward, that this sweaty haste
> Doth make the night joint labourer with the day?
>
> (1.1.70–77)

Against this backdrop, and his own reluctance to take bloody revenge, Hamlet asks the actors if they remember a play that tells the story of the merciless and bloody sacking of Troy by the Greeks. He recites a passage from the play, setting the scene of Pyrrhus's ruthless butchering of the town's population and the apocalyptic burning of Troy:

> ... Head to foot
> Now is he total gules,[33] horridly tricked
> With blood of fathers, mothers, daughters, sons,
> Baked and impasted with the parching streets,
> That lend a tyrannous and damnèd light
> To their lord's murder.
>
> (2.2.437–442)

Hamlet asks the actor first to recount the heinous deed of Pyrrhus, "Priam's slaughter" (2.2.429), and then recite the part that tells of the grief of Priam's wife, Hecuba, over his murder.

Apart from drawing parallels with Claudius's villainy, Hamlet knows Pyrrhus is a mindless destroyer: Troy is burned to the ground and its population killed for no reason other than the greed and bestiality of the conquerors. This is the true face of war. It is pointless and supremely inhumane.

When Fortinbras appears on his way through Denmark to

Poland, Hamlet asks a captain what the contention is in Poland. The answer he gets is revealing:

> We go to gain a little patch of ground
> That hath in it no profit but the name.
> To pay five ducats, five, I would not farm it.
>
> (4.4.17–19)

Hamlet's reply comments on the nature of war:

> This is th' impostume of much wealth and peace,
> That inward breaks and shows no cause without
> Why the man dies.
>
> (4.4.26–28)

Curiously, it is immediately after this comment that Hamlet seems to be energised in his purpose of seeking revenge for his father's death—by Fortinbras and his men fighting for "an eggshell" (4.4.52). Hamlet is opposed to mindless war and senseless bloodshed. It is partly what keeps him from killing Claudius. The futility of bloodshed and war is an important theme in *Hamlet*.

THE EQUALITY OF HUMANKIND

Perhaps the most important theme of all is the repeated emphasis on human equality, which is connected with all other themes mentioned above. All are an expression of the humanist worldview.

Hamlet insists throughout the play that he is not interested in rank and status but that he desires friendship, love, and genuine loyalty. This is his measure of humanity. He seeks this from the watchmen at the start of the play, he emphasises it with Horatio, he treats the actors as his friends, and he considers the gravediggers his equals. He does not find such honesty in Ophelia or in Claudius's other pawns.

This profound understanding of human equality, regardless of social rank, is elaborated in Hamlet's interpretation of death as the great equaliser. This theme is developed in his comments following the death of Polonius, and it is most fully articulated in the scene with the gravediggers.

4. THE DRAMA OF IT ALL

Just how Shakespeare makes *Hamlet* a thrilling theatrical experience can be studied in his use of a variety of dramatic devices. Among these are:

DOUBLING[34] AND FOILS[35]

- Hamlet and Horatio are two humanist scholars who agree on such ideas as a scientific method, the Renaissance image of humankind, the fundamental equality of humans.
- Hamlet and Fortinbras are both sons of slain kings. In both cases an uncle has replaced the father on the throne. Fortinbras is a foil to Hamlet, in that he continues the feudal tradition. He represents Hamlet's generation without humanist learning.
- Laertes too is a foil. He seeks immediate revenge for his father's death and his sister's insanity. However, when he is given the opportunity to do so, and is in fact urged on by Claudius, he begins to share Hamlet's hesitations. Both young men refer to their conscience as moral guide. They forgive each

other. Laertes is therefore closer to the humanist tradition than Fortinbras.

CONTRAST[36]

- These foils of Hamlet, Laertes and Fortinbras are also examples of contrast. They illustrate the different avenues open to people at Hamlet's time—the transition from feudalism to early capitalism. Added to this is of course the Machiavellian road, represented by Claudius.
- Much dramatic effect is also achieved in the sequencing of scenes: terrifying ghost scenes are alternated with double-faced courtly scenes; the scene where Claudius and Laertes plot Hamlet's death is followed by the humorous gravedigger scene, followed by Ophelia's funeral procession.

DRAMATIC IRONY[37]

- This is often found in soliloquies and asides, where a character reveals private plans to the audience that will influence events. The spectators then know more than the characters in the play, which creates suspense. One case in point is the ghost's demand of revenge from Hamlet.
- Hamlet's "madness" is also an example of dramatic irony, as only very few know this is put on and that Hamlet is perfectly sane. This makes for some funny scenes.
- It can be situational irony, for instance the use of the play, *The Murder of Gonzalo*, where Hamlet, Horatio and the audience know to expect a major reaction from Claudius, which comes as a complete surprise to the other characters.
- It can also manifest itself as non-verbal irony, as in the case of

Ophelia handing characters flowers that attribute certain qualities to them, reflecting their guilt or weaknesses.

IMAGERY[38]

• There is a pervasive sense of rottenness and disease: Denmark is referred to as a garden that is not looked after, that is overgrown with weeds. Hamlet refers to Claudius as a cancer and to Fortinbras's wars as tumours.
• Related to this are several images suggesting the plague.
• Ophelia's language of wild flowers picks up on the imagery of weeds, commenting on this ironically.

MOTIF[39]

• Madness: Hamlet's feigned madness is part of his disguise but also allows him to articulate truths.
• Ophelia's madness is a manifestation of total loss.

FORESHADOWING[40]

• The watchmen, Horatio and Hamlet all feel that the appearance of King Hamlet's ghost forebodes bad news for Denmark.
• The discussion with the gravediggers foreshadows Hamlet's own death and burial, along with Laertes, Gertrude, and Claudius, in this very graveyard.
• Cannon shots at the end of the play foreshadow the nature of Fortinbras's rule as new King of Denmark.

5. CLOSE FOCUS: THE GRAVEDIGGER SCENE

ACT 5, SCENE 1[41]

Act 5 opens with the first appearance of working people as independently acting persons on the world stage. They are two gravediggers discussing corruption in society, their own worth, and the equality of all humankind. The significance of this can hardly be overestimated.

The scene begins with the gravediggers, entirely on their own and completely self-sufficient, chatting and commenting on social injustice. Suicide victims were not normally buried in a churchyard in those days. The gravediggers comment how this rule does not apply to the nobility and how lawyers ensure this: "Crowner's quest[42] law" (20). They laugh at their own logic that therefore the wealthy have more reason to kill themselves than their ordinary fellow-Christians: "great folk should have countenance in this world to drown or hang themselves more than their *even Christian*" (24–26; emphasis added).

This train of thought quickly moves on to an astonishing expression of self-respect: "There is no ancient gentleman but gardeners, ditchers, and grave-makers. They hold up Adam's profession" (28–29). A connection is made by the gravedigger to the Peasant Revolt of 1381, where one of the leaders, John Ball, asked in a sermon: "When Adam delved and Eva span, who was then the gentleman?"[43] Ball advocated the social equality of all. The gravedigger develops this idea. A gentleman's coat of arms is swiftly reinterpreted to mean physical arms as the only arms worth having. They enable people to work and to build.

This in turn leads to banter about a gravedigger building the most permanent of housing: "The houses that he makes last till doomsday" (54–55). The working people in this scene are given even more space than the players beforehand. They are more clearly drawn as individuals. They have a direct and unromanticised relationship with their job, which Hamlet and Horatio comment on. They are superbly confident. The humour they bring onto the stage acts as a comic relief to the mounting tension of the main plot, but it is far more than that: it is a manifestation of the absolute integrity of the gravediggers.

The gravedigger's song anticipates his conversation with Hamlet. It is about youth, ageing, and death, functioning as a foreshadowing chorus.[44]

The gravediggers are even more radical in their understanding of death than Hamlet. Hamlet had displayed a profoundly materialist[45] concept of death at the time of Polonius's demise, yet he is taken aback at first by the unceremonious treatment of human bones by the singing gravedigger.

The gravedigger's throwing about of skulls, irrespective of whose they might be, parallels Hamlet's earlier statements about the levelling role of death, suggesting the natural equality of all humankind. This is another instance of *doubling*, or restating of an idea. In addition, Shakespeare is making the point that the working gravediggers have reached the same insights as the university-educated Hamlet by their work, their lives, and independent thinking.

Hamlet vents his disgust at double standards with Horatio (more doubling, as the gravediggers just discussed the same) before he addresses the gravedigger.

Hamlet is in for a surprise when he begins talking to the gravedigger. This man is his equal in the important matters of punning speech, honesty, and absoluteness.

The theme of a fundamental common humanity is underlined as Hamlet joins the gravedigger, along with Horatio. They all occupy the same space and have a scientific discussion about the process of decomposition, linking it with Hamlet's comments about death at the time of Polonius's demise.

At this time, in the graveyard, we see representatives of the working people together with the humanist prince and the humanist middle-class scholar. They understand each other fully and without hierarchy. At the level of language they are equals: no-one can outwit the gravediggers. Basic human equality is emphasised again, and social criticism made, as they toss around the skulls.

When Hamlet is given the skull of Yorick, the court jester of his childhood, he vividly recalls him and alludes once more to the perfectibility of humankind as well as the material nature of death.

Hamlet, Horatio and the gravediggers are natural allies. There are only a few occasions in the play when Hamlet feels relaxed and with his own kind of person—a person of integrity and honesty. This scene is one of those moments; another is when he interacts with the players.

When asking ourselves why Hamlet finds it difficult to set right his time, we must consider what allies are available to him. They are all gathered in the churchyard. It becomes clear that his undertaking is all but impossible, and that a solution lies in the future.

It would be another forty years or so before similar characters would be a strong enough force in English society to challenge and execute their king, or form movements whose objectives included a more just and equal society.

In this context the function of the scene within the tragedy becomes extraordinarily clear. It expands our understanding of

Hamlet's alternatives, even if their time has not yet come. In this episode, on the edges, even remote from the main plot, social inequality and human equality are discussed by those whose task it will be to set right the time by revolutionary upheaval.

6. NOTE THE LANGUAGE

As in all his plays, in *Hamlet* Shakespeare mainly uses blank verse in iambic pentameter,[46] and prose. Blank verse is usually reserved for the speech of the nobility. Hamlet uses this with his mother and always in his soliloquies.[47]

> How weary, stale, flat, and unprofitable
> Seem to me all the uses of this world!
> Fie on't, ah fie! 'Tis an unweeded garden
> That grows to seed. Things rank and gross in nature
> Possess it merely.
>
> (1.2.133–137)

The fact that Hamlet never strays into prose in his soliloquies manifests the fact that his "madness" is put on.

He speaks to the players, to Horatio, Rosencrantz and Guildenstern and the gravediggers in prose, as opposed to the blank verse reserved for the court. Some of the most famous lines in Shakespeare are indeed in prose, because they are set in a particular situation. Here Hamlet tells the actors what he considers the purpose of theatre:

> . . . the purpose of playing, whose end, both at the first and now, was and is to hold, as 'twere, the mirror up to nature, to show virtue her own feature, scorn her own

image, and the very age and body of the time his form and pressure.[48]

(3.2.18–22)

Prose is also typically used for characters of a lower class or indeed for the mad. Hamlet speaks in prose when he is with the actors and gravediggers as well as with friends. Here he is addressing Horatio in the graveyard, as he observes the gravediggers tossing about skulls:

> And now my Lady Worm's,[49] chapless[50] and knocked about the mazard[51] with a sexton's spade. Here's fine revolution, an we had the trick to see 't. Did these bones cost no more the breeding but to play at loggets[52] with them? Mine ache to think on 't.
>
> (5.1.81–85)

It is an expression of madness when he uses prose to communicate with the people at court:

> If thou dost marry, I'll give thee this plague for thy dowry. Be thou as chaste as ice, as pure as snow, thou shalt not escape calumny. Get thee to a nunnery,[53] go. Farewell. (3.1.136–138)

It goes without saying that Ophelia, genuinely mad, also speaks in prose:

> There's rosemary, that's for remembrance. Pray you, love, remember. And there is pansies, that's for thoughts.
>
> (4.5.175–176)

THE BEAUTY OF THE LANGUAGE

In this passage Hamlet confronts his humanist ideal of humankind and the world with the reality he encounters at Elsinore. Shakespeare lets Hamlet pitch the two visions against each other. I here mark the juxtaposition with italic and bold type:

> . . . **this goodly frame, the earth,** seems to me *a sterile promontory*[54]; **this most excellent canopy, the air— look you, this brave o'erhanging firmament, this majestical roof fretted with golden fire**—why, it appears no other thing to me than *a foul and pestilent congregation of vapours.*[55] **What a piece of work is a man! How noble in reason, how infinite in faculty! In form and moving how express and admirable! In action how like an angel, in apprehension how like a god! The beauty of the world. The paragon of animals.** And yet, to me, what is *this quintessence of dust? Man delights not me. No, nor woman neither.*
>
> (2.2.289–305)

The contrasts are striking. Shakespeare invites the audience to imagine the beauty of life only to dash it with images of the plague. There is a rising tide of beauty-filled images. They grow in complexity and length, while their antitheses are far less vivid and vibrant. The exquisiteness of the images describing the potential beauty of life and nature make them memorable. Memorability is a defining feature of beauty in art.

7. THE ENDING

The play ends with the deaths of Hamlet, Laertes, Claudius, and Gertrude. The Machiavellian villain is destroyed, but so is the humanist successor to the throne, Hamlet. The question arises, Who should now take the throne?

Hamlet and Laertes both had the love and vote of the people at some stage in the play: Claudius says of Hamlet, "He's loved of the distracted multitude" (4.3.4) and the "rabble" call: "Choose we! Laertes shall be king!" (4.5.100–104). But neither Hamlet nor Laertes is available at the end of the play.

The question of succession occupies Hamlet's mind to his dying breath, when he appoints Fortinbras: "But I do prophesy the election lights | On Fortinbras. He has my dying voice" (5.2.357–358). Fortinbras accepts. This way, Norwegian territories are restored to him and he now adds Denmark. No doubt he feels there is justice in this:

> For me, with sorrow I embrace my fortune.
> I have some rights of memory in this kingdom,
> Which now to claim my vantage doth invite me.
>
> (5.2.392–394)

What kind of a king Fortinbras will make is written into his actions in the play. His occupation is war, irrespective of the sacrifice it entails. In some ways he appears like Pyrrhus, arriving with "warlike noise" (5.2.351) at the end of the play.

Why does Hamlet choose him—Hamlet who was so critical of Fortinbras's senseless invasion of Poland; Hamlet who abhors war?

The gravedigger scene shows who Hamlet's allies are. None of these are ready to reign in Denmark in his spirit. Fortinbras has a certain interest in regaining Norwegian lands and adding to these. Perhaps this way a war against Denmark can be avoided.

One thing is clear: Fortinbras will be a king of the old kind; he will continue in the tradition of Hamlet's father. He is no modern Machiavellian. Possibly this means political stability in the short term. However, history cannot be rolled back. The people of Denmark have endorsed both Hamlet and Laertes, young men with a conscience. They will remember them as potential rulers. Their memory will live on, as Horatio is given the task of keeping it alive.

The people of Denmark are heard throughout the play. They appear in groups as the actors and gravediggers. They are quoted for their opinions; they are a voice to be reckoned with.[56]

Hamlet was written about 1600. In 1649 the people of England executed Charles I. Dissatisfaction with the king, and radical intellectual questioning, ultimately led to the English Revolution.[57] Manifestations of the revolutionary potential inherent in this upheaval were the movements of the lower middle-class Levellers and the Diggers. The Diggers envisaged a future in which all humans were equal and a new social order based on reason and science.

8. CONCLUSIONS: WHAT IS THE TRAGEDY?

Hamlet's downfall is caused by the times in which he lives, Shakespeare's time of transition from the old feudal order to the early capitalism of the Elizabethan-Jacobean epoch. These times have produced a new type of man: Claudius. He manipulates all around him. He deceives people about his true nature as a ruthless politician who wants the most powerful post in Denmark.

To set right his time and to get rid of Claudius, Hamlet is forced into behaving in ways that contradict his humanist understanding. He is terribly torn between bowing to the old feudal code, employing Machiavellian methods of deception, and his own Renaissance humanism, which considers conscience the moral measure.

Hamlet's humanist world view is his inner human substance. It proves impossible for him to maintain this core under the circumstances of his time and the Danish court. The conflict he experiences between his efforts to set right his time and the impossibility of doing so on his own humanist terms cannot be resolved.

The sympathy, or pity, evoked in the audience arises from Hamlet's human potential, which in other times and circumstances would contribute to humanising society. The rift between what is and what might be creates a sense of possible change—that the times can be set right. This change to a humanist society points into the future—even our own future. The play uncovers alternatives to the society of its time and encourages thinking about ways to achieve this.

The loss of humanist philosophy as a determining factor in kingship, which would have come about with young Hamlet's accession to the throne, the loss of Hamlet's kindness, scientific insight and sense of human equality are the tragedy of this play. This loss evokes both our pity and our grief.

FOOTNOTES

17 Revenge is for retaliation and often begets a cycle of violence, whereas retribution is for restoring justice.

18 The word "kind" is important to Shakespeare. In this play, and in others, it means both "kindness" and being of the same kind or species.

19 Marlowe's father was a shoemaker.

20 A Machiavellian is a ruthless, unprincipled egotist in pursuit of power, wealth, and status. He is willing to use any kind of deceit to achieve his aims and does not shrink from murder. See chapter I above, "The context, humanism, and Machiavellianism."

21 symptomatic of the plague.

22 for flattery and deceit.

23 for ingratitude.

24 for repentance.

25 for innocence.

26 for faithfulness.

27 (buttercups), for ingratitude.

28 stinging.

29 innocence.

30 sexual love.

31 He uses the same word, "conscience," that is Hamlet's measure of conduct.

32 This role was played by Shakespeare himself.

33 red.

34 reinforcing a theme by emphasis.

35 reinforcing a theme by contrast.

36 To heighten awareness of opposites, the specific nature of one is played off against that of another.

37 This is a device whereby the playwright allows the audience to know more than the characters.

38 This underlines the main themes of a play in a non-verbal manner.

39 A motif in literature is a recurring device that has a symbolic significance and underlines and expands the main themes.

40 Foreshadowing is a kind of dramatic irony where the full truth of a statement becomes apparent only with hindsight.

41 Strictly speaking, the gravedigger scene is the first part of act 5, scene 1, which continues with Ophelia's burial.

42 coroner's inquest.

43 These words, spoken at the time of the peasant rising in a sermon at Blackheath, near London, became legendary. The next sentence is: "From the beginning all men by nature were created equal." John Ball deduced the equality of humankind from their common descent from Adam.

44 The chorus in ancient Greek theatre commented on the play's central themes.

45 Materialist here means entirely physical, without reference to a soul.

46 Iambic pentameter is poetry written in lines of ten syllables with five beats. This sounds like a heartbeat or a horse galloping; it is a basic human rhythm: da-DUM da-DUM da-DUM da-DUM da-DUM.

47 We distinguish between metre and rhythm. Metre is the underlying pattern of stressed and unstressed syllables—in Shakespeare mainly (iambic) blank verse. Rhythm is a feature of natural spoken language, which can subtly shift the metre. The interaction between metre and rhythm accentuates the meaning and creates tension in the spoken verse, so that it sounds like natural speech.

48 Emphasis added.

49 Now these bones belong to the worms.

50 With the lower jawbone missing.

51 Mazard: skull.

52 A game formerly played in England in which players threw pieces of wood at a stake in the ground—an old-fashioned type of bowling.

53 A convent; but in Shakespeare's day this word was also used for a brothel.

54 Bodily swelling, as is symptomatic of bubonic plague.

55 "Pestilent vapours" is a reference to the airborne spread of the plague.

56 Humanist writers such as Erasmus had begun thinking about necessary changes for a better society a century before Shakespeare. Erasmus outlined the qualities needed in good leaders in his writings. Thomas More wrote a book entitled *Utopia* in which he explored the potential for an equal society, without hierarchies. This is the humanist intellectual context within which Shakespeare writes.

57 This time is often referred to as the Civil War in England. I adopt the term used by Christopher Hill and other historians, as it best reflects this time's pivotal nature in the transition from feudalism to capitalism.

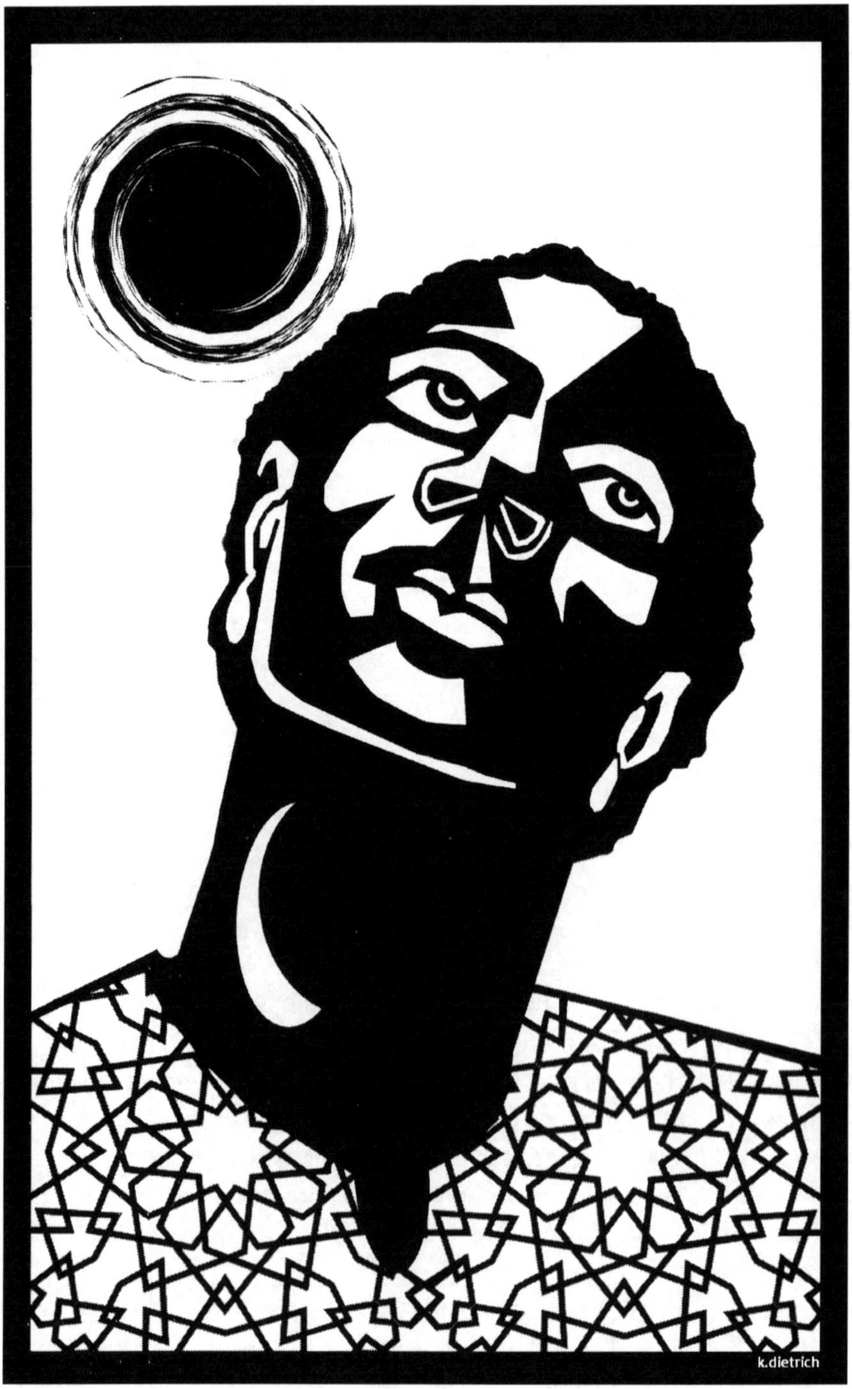
k.dietrich

CHAPTER III

OTHELLO (1603)

> *"And when I love thee not*
> *Chaos is come again"*
> —Act 3, scene 3

Cyprus was a possession of the Republic of Venice for a little more than eighty years. This ended with the Turkish takeover in 1570, an event that fell into Shakespeare's lifetime. This war is the historical setting for *Othello*.

Othello is the commander of the Venetian forces defending Cyprus against the Ottoman Empire. However, the play is not about this historical event. The *Othello* plot is based on one of a collection of Cinthio's stories,[58] *Un Capitano Moro*. So here too, as in many of his plays, Shakespeare uses and uniquely changes an existing plot to explore issues relating to his own time.

1. THE PLOT

The play opens against the backdrop of a Turkish threat against

Venetian-controlled Cyprus. A Turkish fleet is under way, and military intervention is needed urgently. The Duke of Venice has called an emergency night-time meeting of the Senate. The Senate has sent messengers to look for Othello, whom they wish to send out as commander in chief of the Venetian troops to defeat the Ottoman threat.

However, while this is going on, and before the audience become aware of it, Iago, the play's villain, is introduced. Othello has not promoted him to the position of lieutenant—second in command. Instead this honour is awarded to Cassio, and Iago remains a mere "ancient" (i.e. ensign or flag-bearer), a junior officer.

Iago's all but first words announce that he hates Othello. From this develops his campaign for Othello's destruction. He gets Rodrigo, a "friend" from whom he borrows much money, to waken Desdemona's father, Brabantio, in the middle of the night. Together they slur his daughter and Othello, who have just married in secret. Brabantio is enraged over this and is out for revenge. He finds Othello at the same time as the Senate's messengers. They all go to the meeting of the Senate.

In the scene before the Senate there is at first talk of the Turkish threat. Brabantio and Othello arrive. Brabantio brings his accusations against Othello before the Duke, who listens to both parties and then calls for Desdemona to speak. After hearing both Desdemona and Othello, the Duke tells Brabantio to accept the marriage.

Othello consents to the military commission, and Desdemona requests that she be allowed to travel with him. It is arranged that Iago will accompany her to Cyprus, along with his wife, Emilia, as Desdemona's attendant.

Iago ensnares the naïve Rodrigo in a project ostensibly to

win Desdemona's affections with money when she tires of Othello. Left alone on stage, Iago discloses his true plan to ruin Othello by making him jealous.

Act 2 opens in Cyprus. Desdemona, Emilia, Iago and Cassio have arrived, but a storm has delayed Othello and has sunk the Turkish fleet. Before Othello arrives, Iago reveals his profound cynicism about humankind. In this instance he also voices unqualified negative generalisations about all of womankind.

Othello arrives, and Iago tells Rodrigo to pick a row with Cassio. In another soliloquy, Iago presents the audience with a detailed description of how he will cause havoc and destroy Othello's happiness through distrust.

Iago loses no time. He makes Cassio drunk, which leads to a fight with Rodrigo. This row escalates, and Othello appears, demanding order and an explanation from Iago about who started the brawl. In this scene Iago appears to Othello to be honest and trustworthy.

As act 2 closes, Iago, in two more soliloquies, tells the spectators of his next steps against Othello: he will "pour this pestilence into his ear" (2.3.336), and of Desdemona's "goodness make the net | That shall enmesh them all" (2.3.341–342).

At Iago's suggestion, Cassio pleads with Desdemona to help him regain Othello's confidence. She speaks to Othello on his behalf.

Iago moves forward with his intrigue. During an insinuating talk with Othello, in which Iago suggests that Desdemona is unfaithful to him, he gradually changes the balance of power in their relationship. He makes Othello insecure and begins to tell him what to do.

Othello abandons his doubts about Desdemona immediately

he sees her. Fatefully, Desdemona drops a handkerchief given to her by Othello as she tends to her husband's headache. Emilia picks it up and gives it to Iago, because he has asked her for it a number of times. When Desdemona confides in Emilia that the handkerchief is lost, Emilia does not disclose what happened to it.

Iago returns for another psychological onslaught, which leaves Othello convinced of Desdemona's adultery and with thoughts of killing Cassio as well as Desdemona. He has listened to and believed Iago's lies about Cassio and rages with Desdemona when she cannot produce the handkerchief, thus apparently confirming Iago's insinuations.

Iago contrives a situation in which Othello overhears a conversation with Cassio suggesting that he is laughing at the "prostitute" Desdemona (in fact Cassio is speaking of Bianca). Othello's rage and murderous thoughts focus increasingly on Desdemona.

Desdemona appears with Lodovico, who brings Othello a letter from the Duke, recalling him to Venice and asking him to install Cassio as governor of Cyprus. As Desdemona expresses happiness at this turn of events, Othello strikes her publicly. Lodovico is shocked, saying that this is out of keeping with Othello's reputation.

Next Othello seeks out Emilia to question her about Desdemona. Emilia strongly defends Desdemona's fidelity and integrity. However, when Desdemona appears, Othello viciously and vilely accuses her of adultery, and does not allow her to defend herself.

As he leaves, Iago comes in, and Emilia develops a growing suspicion of her husband's involvement in the crisis. She makes this clear, but Iago tells her to keep quiet.

In contrast, Desdemona still believes in Iago's honesty and expresses her grief to him over Othello's behaviour.

Rodrigo also seems to be grasping the fact that Iago is exploiting him, stating: "your words and performances are no kin together" (4.2.190–191). Iago once again manipulates the situation and sets up Rodrigo to kill Cassio that night.

Desdemona has already asked Emilia to put her wedding sheets on the bed and now requests that in the event of her death these sheets be used for her shroud. Emilia tries to get Desdemona to overcome her melancholic, indeed death-fearing mood by rationalising.

The final act begins with Iago organising Rodrigo's ultimately unsuccessful assassination of Cassio, leading to the death of Rodrigo. Once again Iago manages to emerge as the impartial mediator taking charge of the situation.

This scene is followed by the final one of Othello in his and Desdemona's bedchamber. As often when face to face with Desdemona, Othello is in doubt whether to really believe in her dishonesty and to proceed with her murder. However, he wakes her with a kiss, commands her to pray, then smothers her, giving her no opportunity to answer his accusations with proof to the contrary. Iago's claims and the handkerchief are his only evidence.

Emilia rushes in as she hears Desdemona's death cries and establishes there and then, with growing horror, that Othello's actions were based exclusively on her husband's insinuations.

As Iago and others join them in the chamber, Emilia reveals Iago's guilt—and he stabs her to death. Othello is beside himself and commits suicide. Lodovico nominates Cassio as lord governor of Cyprus and charges him with the responsibility of serving justice on Iago.

2. WHO ARE THE CHARACTERS?

OTHELLO

It is hard to imagine just how startling it must have been for the Jacobean theatregoers to be presented with a black general—and one held in high esteem by the government of Venice. Although there had been some black nobles and military leaders in Europe,[59] the few black people living in London from Tudor times were almost all servants. In January 1601 Queen Elizabeth I issued a proclamation expelling all "Blackmoores" from England. So Othello, the highly regarded general, is clearly marked not only as an outsider but also as very exceptional and a challenge to the prejudices and stereotypes of society.

Othello is portrayed as noble. He is of a royal family, and his ability as a military leader is unparalleled:

> ... for he's embarked
> With such loud reason to the Cyprus wars
> (Which even now stand in act) that, for their souls,
> Another of his fathom they have none
> To lead their business.
>
> (Iago, 1.1.152–156)

He is reasonable and confident:

> ... Let him do his spite.
> My services which I have done the signiory
> Shall out-tongue his complaints.
>
> (1.2.17–19)

Othello's behaviour when confronted with Brabantio shows

that he is calm, in control, and good at defusing a crisis. Later, in Cyprus, he stops the fight between Rodrigo and Cassio simply by his authority, showing true leadership qualities in his sense of responsibility for law and order:

> ... What, in a town of war
> Yet wild, the people's hearts brimful of fear,
> To manage private and domestic quarrel?
> In night, and on the court and guard of safety?
> 'Tis monstrous.
>
> (2.3.200–204)

In a beautifully poetic speech in act 1, scene 3, Othello makes the most extensive statement about himself, his background, and his love for Desdemona; it ends:

> She loved me for the dangers I had passed,
> And I loved her that she did pity them.
>
> (1.3.168–169)

All this is established in the first two acts of the play. It makes the downfall of Othello all the more shocking. How is it possible? Othello, for all his confidence and control in military situations, is completely unused to modern European civilian society. Specifically, he is not prepared for Machiavellian deception. Othello's values are honesty, loyalty, and respect. He cannot imagine that these may be twisted and undermined and that people can be driven insane in psychological warfare. His humane core is his absolute sincerity and his trust in people: his humanity.

This is what Iago desires to undermine. Once Othello's mind

becomes unhinged by Iago's insinuations, all his goodness is turned into ugliness. He becomes the opposite of what he was: he is irrational and will not allow Desdemona to reason with him.

He who had laughed at the idea of having used "magic" to attract Desdemona now uses superstition to frighten her when she admits she has misplaced the handkerchief.

> ... There's magic in the web of it.
> A sibyl, that had numbered in the world
> The sun to course two hundred compasses,
> In her prophetic fury sewed the work.
> The worms were hallowed that did breed the silk,
> And it was dyed in mummy which the skillful
> Conserved of maidens' hearts.
>
> (3.4.66–72)

And he becomes incoherent in his loss of control:

> ... they belie her! Lie with her—that's fulsome. Handkerchief—confessions—handkerchief! To confess, and be hanged for his labour. First, to be hanged, and then to confess—I tremble at it. Nature would not invest herself in such shadowing passion without some instruction. It is not words that shake me thus. Pish! Noses, ears, and lips. Is't possible? Confess!—Handkerchief!—Oh, devil!—
>
> (4.1.34–41)

The contempt with which Iago suggests Desdemona and Cassio having sex "as prime as goats, as hot as monkeys"

(3.3.411) ingrains itself deeply in Othello's mind and emerges in his incoherent rage as "Goats and monkeys" (4.1.258).

Sadly, the once-confident and expansive Othello begins to think of himself in animal terms: "A hornèd man's a monster and a beast" (4.1.59). He is reduced by Iago to self-loathing.

This is in stark contrast to the stories he told that had won Desdemona's heart. Othello is destroyed; "chaos has come again" (3.3.92) to take the place that had been inhabited by love.

As this happens, Othello's language loses its humanity, its poetry, and becomes brutal and vile as he accuses Desdemona of infidelity:

> Was this fair paper, this most goodly book,
> Made to write "whore" upon? What committed?
> Committed? O thou public commoner!
> I should make very forges of my cheeks
> That would to cinders burn up modesty
> Did I but speak thy deeds.
> ...
> Impudent strumpet!
>
> (4.2.75–85)

His language flattens with his state of mind—becomes less global. In his last speech Othello returns to a more culturally encompassing vision:

> Speak of me as I am.
> ...
> Of one not easily jealous, but being wrought,
> Perplexed in the extreme. Of one whose hand,

> Like the base Indian, threw a pearl away
> Richer than all his tribe. Of one whose subdued eyes,
> Albeit unused to the melting mood,
> Drop tears as fast as the Arabian trees
> Their medicinal gum.
>
> (5.2.358–367)

Like Hamlet when he asks Laertes for forgiveness, Othello pleads that he was beside himself.

IAGO

Iago is the character in all four tragedies we are concerned with here who is most clearly cast in the tradition of Vice in the medieval morality plays. The Vice in those plays was irredeemably evil—and entertainingly so—always seeking to capture the soul of Everyman. He had no particular cause to be evil: it was his nature as the envoy from Hell. Vice spoke to the audience in asides and soliloquies, making it part of his plans and watching along with them how the other characters walk into his traps. In one sense he was the puppet-master. Iago is exactly like this; and he frequently refers to his hellish nature and plans:

> ... Divinity of hell!
> When devils will the blackest sins put on
> They do suggest at first with heavenly shows
> As I do now.
>
> (2.3.330–333)

Yet he is no medieval stereotype or incarnation of evil in quite the same sense. Yes, the playgoers would have seen him in that cast, but they also understood that Iago was a real, dangerous modern version of this. Amusingly, Iago is—like Niccolò Machiavelli—from Florence.

Right at the start of the play Iago declares his deceptive nature:

> Were I the Moor, I would not be Iago.
> In following him, I follow but myself.
> Heaven is my judge, not I for love and duty,
> But seeming so, for my peculiar end.
>
> (1.1.59–62)

Iago is dishonest and cynical:

> The Moor is of a free and open nature
> That thinks men honest that but seem to be so,
> And will as tenderly be led by th' nose
> As asses are.
>
> (1.3.390–393)

He is the true opposite of Othello in this cynicism. Othello is also diametrically opposed to Iago in his capacity for love. Iago describes Othello as a "Barbary horse" (1.1.115) and bestialises him:

> ... an old black ram
> Is tupping your white ewe. Arise, arise,
> Awake the snorting citizens with the bell
> Or else the devil will make a grandsire of you.
>
> (1.1.90–93)

Typically for an extremely self-interested person, Iago has no friends or relationships of equality with other human beings. Loyalty and love for another person undermines egotism. Genuine friendship and love possess the quality of human kindness. Iago rejects these. He is married to Emilia, but he has no regard for her. When she comprehends his deadly intrigue and reveals this he kills her without hesitation.

Iago is a skilled manipulator. His chief weapon is language: he manipulates by insinuation. (This will be explored in more detail when we take a close look at act 3, scene 3 below.)

Like most of Shakespeare's representatives of the modern generation, including the Machiavellians, Iago is not superstitious: "we work by wit and not by witchcraft" (2.3.351).

His complete disregard for human life and happiness is demonstrated in his desire to destroy Othello, and also Desdemona. He is the first to suggest to Othello that Desdemona ought to be killed, and how to kill her: "Do it not with poison. Strangle her in her bed" (4.1.197).

The death toll at the end of the play is ultimately Iago's responsibility.

DESDEMONA

Desdemona[60] is a woman of great integrity. Just before the events of the play begin she has married Othello. She has defied her society's norms in an act of love. She says she is drawn to him because "I saw Othello's visage in his mind" (1.3.252).

Desdemona chose a partner independent of rank or any social consideration. She chose him because of his personality, because of the life he had led and the great wonders he shared with her. This is a love that transcends all prejudices, and this makes her a true partner for Othello. She too believes in their love.[61]

When she becomes worried about Othello's behaviour she talks to Emilia about husbands and wives and marital respect. Emilia has been married to Iago and has adopted some of his cynicism about loyalty in human relationships.

Marital relationships are viewed as loveless, and Desdemona's concept of a meeting of minds is turned on its head. She shares Othello's abhorrence of betrayal of the spouse. She does not believe that two wrongs make a right:

> ... Heaven me such uses send,
> Not to pick bad from bad, but by bad mend!
> (4.3.99–100)

Desdemona remains loyal and is incapable of thinking ill of Othello. This leads to her death. She asks him repeatedly to allow her to prove her innocence; Othello will not hear of it, so obsessed is he with Iago's insinuations. This is very different from Desdemona's affirmation of her love for Othello when he calls for her before the Senate. When Desdemona asks for the same favour, Othello will not grant it. Iago has destroyed Othello's reason.

In contrast to Othello, Desdemona's self-esteem remains undamaged.

EMILIA

Emilia is a genuine person and is not afraid of Iago. However, we witness no closeness between them. When he expresses his cynical attitude to women she doesn't let him get away with it: "You shall not write my praise" (2.1.125). She says about husbands:

> ... What is it that they do
> When they change us for others? Is it sport?
> I think it is. And doth affection breed it?
> I think it doth. Is't frailty that thus errs?
> It is so too. And have not we affections,
> Desires for sport, and frailty, as men have?
> Then let them use us well, else let them know,
> The ills we do, their ills instruct us so.
>
> (4.3.91–98)

This view, while it underlines Emilia's independence, also speaks of an absence of loyalty or love in her relationship with Iago.

However, Emilia is unaware of the full extent of Iago's evil. When Cassio approaches her in an effort to appeal to Desdemona for intervention with Othello on his behalf, Emilia comforts him and reassures him. She too is taken in by Iago's deception: "I warrant it grieves my husband, | As if the cause were his" (3.3.3–4).

When she takes Desdemona's handkerchief, she has clearly no idea how this will be abused.

While she is still reasonably loyal to Iago at this point, bringing him the handkerchief because he asked for it, her loyalty is soon strongly on Desdemona's side. When Othello questions her regarding Desdemona's faithfulness, she answers extensively and eloquently:

> I durst, my lord, to wager she is honest,
> Lay down my soul at stake. If you think other
> Remove your thought, it doth abuse your bosom.
> If any wretch have put this in your head

> Let heaven requite it with the serpent's curse
> For if she be not honest, chaste, and true
> There's no man happy. The purest of their wives
> Is foul as slander.
>
> (4.2.13–20)

Here Emilia states her case clearly. She also chides Othello for not being himself, that such jealous thoughts are unworthy of both Desdemona and Othello. In addition, she rightly accuses the "wretch" who put this in Othello's head—and she knows this must have been so. However, at this point she has no notion that it is Iago.

When Emilia overhears Othello's terrible accusations against Desdemona, she calls from behind the locked door: "O good my lord, I would speak a word with you" (5.2.103). After Othello explains his reason for killing Desdemona, Emilia confronts him: "Thou dost belie her, and thou art a devil" (5.2.148).

She soon suspects Iago: "My husband" (5.2.155). She is enraged and very articulate as her suspicion of Iago's foul dealings grows:

> Disprove this villain, if thou be'st a man.
> He says thou told'st him that his wife was false.
> I know thou didst not, thou'rt not such a villain.
> Speak, for my heart is full.
>
> (5.2.185–188)

And she reveals the truth—seeing what no other can see—that her husband is behind all the tragedy. She grasps how the handkerchief has been used to construct this trap:

> O thou dull Moor! That handkerchief thou speak'st of
> I found by fortune and did give my husband.
> For often, with a solemn earnestness—
> More than indeed belonged to such a trifle—
> He begged of me to steal it.
>
> (5.2. 239–243)

This revelation costs Emilia her life. However, with this courageous act, severing herself from her husband in the interest of honesty, she has proved herself second to Desdemona. Like Desdemona, she sacrifices her life for her integrity.

3. WHAT IS THE PLAY ABOUT?

THE STRUGGLE BETWEEN HUMANISM AND MACHIAVELLIANISM

At the heart of this play lies the destruction of love and of human dignity by a Machiavellian force. Love, in Shakespeare's concept of values, enables human beings to transcend the limitations of their world. Love unfetters them and allows them to experience genuine and unconditional affirmation as human beings.

This is what Romeo and Juliet experience for a brief time, and also Othello and Desdemona. In both cases the villainy and violence of society crush their love, and the lovers are destroyed.

The measure of the lovers' appreciation of their special being is always expressed in heightened poetic language.[62] This is how they experience the world: special, new, and beautiful.

Iago is the polar opposite to Othello. He represents essential hatred of humankind. His main object throughout the play is to destroy happiness and love. He reduces love to vulgarly presented sex. Any show of kindness from Iago is insincere and displayed for an ulterior purpose. Iago sets out to destroy the dignity, humanity and capacity for love in Othello. He knows that by destroying Othello's love for Desdemona he is destroying his inner core and thereby his whole person.

Even Emilia cannot conceive of a mutually loving relationship. In her speech defending the rights of women to extramarital relationships she bases this on an eye-for-an-eye argument. Desdemona cannot support this stance.

Othello expresses what love means to him when he cries out, "But I do love thee! And when I love thee not | Chaos is come again" (3.3.91–92). Love has become Othello's principle of order. A world without love has lost all meaning for him. Iago's machinations have brought chaos to Othello, and he loses control. A world based on the principle of love as Othello and Desdemona understand it is a world commensurate with fundamental human needs: equality, cherishing, and affirmation. It requires a society that is not defined by money or status. In this sense it reaches into a utopian future.

THE EQUALITY OF HUMANKIND

The equality of humankind is linked to the theme of love. Othello's and Desdemona's love is based on complete acceptance of human equality. To emphasise this, Shakespeare uses characters from vastly different places in the world. He underlines their common humanity by giving them different skin colours. He makes the black Othello a highly regarded general and invests both lovers with the same understanding of love that transcends all prejudice.

THE INTEGRITY OF WOMEN

The integrity of women is an important theme in Othello and linked to the idea of human equality. Both Desdemona and Emilia are confident in their views and are not afraid to voice them.

Desdemona appears in a trial-like situation before the Senate of Venice early on in the play to defend her choice of Othello for husband. She also displays sagacity in her argument with Othello over when he might resolve the problem with Cassio, and challenges Iago's cynicism about women. Even when in fear of her life as Othello prepares to kill her she demands time, reflection, evidence, and the right to defend herself.

Emilia is an equally confident person and well able to defend herself. She grows enormously in her fearless revelation of Iago's guilt, her accusation against Othello, and her defence of Desdemona's absolute honesty.

Together, Emilia and Desdemona embody Renaissance women of the highest integrity. They are peerless in the play.

4. THE DRAMA OF IT ALL

DRAMATIC DEVICES

The story is more or less told by Iago, the modern devil-like Vice. His many soliloquies and asides draw in the audience, keeping them ahead of the other characters and events at all times. It makes for an exciting dramatic experience and reveals Iago as the puppet-master.

DOUBLING[63] AND FOILS[64]

- There are three couples: Othello and Desdemona, Iago and Emilia, Cassio and Bianca. In each case we see different relationships between lovers, both loving and unloving.
- Emilia doubles Desdemona as a woman of courage and integrity.

CONTRAST[65]

- There is a chasm between Iago's words and his real intention.
- There is a telling contrast between Cassio's dismissal of Bianca's jealousy as irrational when she is given the handkerchief to copy and Othello's raging jealousy sparked by the same handkerchief.
- More contrast arises from the sequencing of scenes: for example, when Othello becomes consumed with jealousy and begins contemplating Desdemona's murder, she affirms to Emilia, when she asks if Othello is jealous, "I think the sun where he was born | Drew all such humours from him" (3.4.27–28).

DRAMATIC IRONY[66]

- The supreme case in point is Iago's running commentary to the audience about how he is steering the catastrophe. Only they know his true plans.
- Another instance is the constant affirmation throughout the play that Iago is honest, when he patently is not.
- An example of situational irony is that directly after Othello

makes his statement about chaos taking the place of love, should love go, Iago appears and has considerable time alone with Othello, when he begins serious insinuations of Desdemona's infidelity. Iago shows how to create chaos, and that he is enjoying it.
- A special form of dramatic irony is when characters express a truth they themselves are unaware of. Here Othello is speaking to Iago, unnerved by Iago's echoing of what he says, insinuating disbelief:

> ... Alas, thou echo'st me,
> As if there were some monster in thy thought
> Too hideous to be shown.
> (3.3.110–112)

This is in fact true, but Othello doesn't know it. Iago and the audience do: it is a different kind of "monster" from the one Othello is thinking of.

- It can also manifest itself as non-verbal irony, for instance in the fact that Othello kills himself with the same knife he used when killing the Turks in an effort to restore order to the Venetian empire.

IMAGERY[67]

- Imagery associated with Heaven and Hell is represented in the colours white and black. In this context it is ironic that Othello, whose skin colour is black, has a divine nature, to be destroyed by Iago, while Iago acknowledges to himself that he is devil-like.
- Bestial imagery is used by Iago to express his cynicism and his

hatred of others, especially Othello. It is instilled in Othello's way of thinking as his mind disintegrates.
• Natural imagery is used by Othello to describe passions.
• The storm the Venetians encounter on their way to Cyprus is imagery for what awaits them there.

MOTIF[68]

• Madness: The dissembling of Othello's mind is a manifestation of his statement that when love is gone, "chaos is come again."

FORESHADOWING[69]

• Iago's soliloquies create enormous dramatic suspense and explicitly foreshadow what unfolds.
• Desdemona's assurance to Cassio that she is a loyal friend to him, that she "shall rather die | Than give thy cause away" (3.3.27–28).
• Desdemona's request that Emilia should put her wedding sheets on her bed and use them for a shroud in the event of her death.

5. CLOSE FOCUS: THE POWER OF MANIPULATION

The pivotal scene of the play is act 3, scene 3. It is also the longest, beginning with Desdemona's promise to help Cassio and ending with Othello's vow of vengeance against her. Between these two points we see Desdemona speak to Othello on Cassio's behalf, the central section of Iago's psychological manipulations of Othello, the loss of the handkerchief, and Iago's use of this as crucial evidence against Desdemona.

At the beginning of this scene Othello is happy and confident in his love for Desdemona; by the end of it he is tormented and ready to kill. This spectacular change has been brought about by Iago. This section of the scene is worth looking at in more detail, as it goes to the heart of the tragedy. It shows the audience in close-up how Iago operates and how he succeeds in destroying Othello.

Iago begins by assuming a certain reluctance to communicate his thoughts. He does this very cleverly in order to arouse Othello's suspicion. As they see Cassio leave Desdemona he comments: "Ha! I like not that" (33), and elaborates "that he would steal away so guilty-like | Seeing you coming" (38–39). Othello and Desdemona then speak and discuss when Othello might hear Cassio.

After Desdemona and Emilia leave, Iago employs insinuating questions and repetitions, suggesting that he is aware of a secret and dishonest side to Cassio:

> Othello: Is he not honest?
> Iago: Honest, my lord?
> Othello: Honest, ay, honest.
> Iago: My lord, for aught I know.
> Othello: What dost thou think?
> Iago: Think, my lord?
> Othello: "Think, my lord?" Alas, thou echo'st me
> As if there were some monster in thy thought
> Too hideous to be shown.
>
> (105–112)

Othello is direct and expects others to be equally so and not to talk in double-meanings. Iago, although he is a great deceiver, knows this about Othello. When Othello says, "Certain, men should be what they seem" (133), Iago replies, "Why then I think Cassio's an honest man" (134). He gets the psychology right, as Othello now begins to doubt his own good sense and asks Iago to "speak to me as to thy thinkings . . . and give thy worst of thoughts | The worst of words" (136–138).

This is exactly what Iago does, not without saying first that it may all be wrong: "I perchance am vicious in my guess" (150). Iago ensnares Othello, stirring his fears more and more, while pretending efforts to the contrary.

Yet he places words clinically to suggest new fears to Othello. It is Iago who first mentions "jealousy" (169), thereby insinuating that there is reason for such to Othello. Othello considers this but rejects it—"she had eyes and chose me" (193)—and says, "I'll see before I doubt, when I doubt, prove" (194).

Iago manipulates this to cause doubt before saying, "I speak not yet of proof" (200). He goes on to strike at Othello's weak spot, that he is an outsider in Venetian society and doesn't know as much as Iago about such matters: "In Venice they do let God see the pranks | They dare not show their husbands" (206–207). And to reinforce this: "She did deceive her father, marrying you" (210).

After all this, Othello has fallen into Iago's trap: "I am bound to thee forever" (217)—"bound," not only grateful but, ironically, tied by him and to him. Othello is moved to tears at this point—"My lord, I see you're moved" (229)—and Iago is confident enough to become seriously offensive towards Othello as he comments on Desdemona's choice of a black man: "One may smell in such a will most rank, | Foul disproportions, thoughts unnatural" (237–238).

It is noteworthy that in leading up to this affront Iago's language becomes influenced by Othello's, thereby making it more persuasive. Indeed in Othello's soliloquy, after Iago exits and Desdemona enters, he has been imbued with this message. The hitherto confident Othello now wonders:

> . . . Haply, for I am black
> And have not those soft parts of conversation
> That chamberers have
> . . .
> She's gone, I am abused, and my relief
> Must be to loathe her.
>
> (267–272)

The downward spiralling of Othello's confidence and self-esteem is dramatically interrupted by an interlude, where Desdemona loses the handkerchief and Emilia picks it up to give to her husband.

When Iago and Othello are on stage again together Iago has noted, "The Moor already changes with my poison" (333), and gloats over the fact that Othello will never sleep soundly again:

> . . . Not poppy nor mandragora
> Nor all the drowsy syrups of the world,
> Shall ever medicine thee to that sweet sleep
> Which thou owedst yesterday.
>
> (338–341)

Again he is assimilating Othello's poetry. Indeed Othello begins not to doubt but to rage, as though he is certain of Desdemona's infidelity. He bids farewell to his military career:

"Farewell! Othello's occupation's gone" (365). By doing so he is taking leave of his identity.

Once more Iago uses Othello's distress to make matters worse and to disguise his dishonesty as honesty. Relentlessly, he moves up a gear and insinuates that he has the proof Othello seeks. He tells him that Cassio spoke in his sleep about his love affair with Desdemona, and then tops it off by mentioning the handkerchief Othello gave her. Othello is now almost driven insane and is set on revenge: "Oh blood, blood, blood!" (458). While Cassio's death is agreed, Iago finishes this amazing scene by placing yet another word to spiral his evil plan to a peak: "But let her live" (481). Othello, who has not thought up to this time of killing Desdemona, falls into this trap too and withdraws to think of "some swift means of death | For the fair devil" (484–485). At the end of this scene Iago has become Othello's de facto general.

In discussing this scene we have concentrated on Iago's manipulation of Othello to turn him in a very short space of time from an expansive, good-natured person into someone beside himself, crippled with insane imaginings fuelled by Iago. Othello moves from being a loving bridegroom to being a puppet of Iago's, ready to kill the person he loves.

6. NOTE THE LANGUAGE

As in all his plays, in *Othello* Shakespeare mainly uses blank verse in iambic pentameter,[70] and prose. Blank verse is usually reserved for the speech of the nobility. In his opening speeches in act 1, scenes 2 and 3, Othello's dignity is emphasised in his measured diction. Blank verse underlines his heroism. [71]

> . . . I fetch my life and being
> From men of royal siege, and my demerits
> May speak unbonneted to as proud a fortune
> As this that I have reached. (1.2.21–24)

Prose is typically used for characters who are either of the lower classes or whose minds have become unhinged. Othello's language disintegrates as a reflection of his mind, as insane jealously, fuelled by Iago, takes hold of him:

> Ay, let her rot and perish and be damned tonight, for she shall not live. No, my heart is turned to stone. I strike it and it hurts my hand. Oh, the world hath not a sweeter creature, she might lie by an emperor's side and command him tasks.
> (4.1.172–176)

THE BEAUTY OF THE LANGUAGE

Here is the passage where Othello speaks before the Senators of how he won Desdemona, telling the adventure of his life:

> Wherein I spoke of most disastrous chances,
> Of moving accidents by flood and field,
> Of hair-breadth 'scapes i' th' imminent deadly breach,
> Of being taken by the insolent foe
> And sold to slavery, of my redemption thence
> And portance in my traveler's history.
> Wherein of antres[72] vast and deserts idle,
> Rough quarries, rocks, hills whose heads touch heaven
> It was my hint to speak—such was the process—

And of the Cannibals that each other eat,
The Anthropophagi,[73] and men whose heads
Do grow beneath their shoulders.[74]

(1.3.135–146)

Othello's language is heroic in this piece. He emerges as a hero from these tales, which are hinted at just in single phrases. Each phrase represents a disastrous experience on land or water: narrow escapes in deadly battles, being sold into slavery and being released from it.

From this personal history Othello moves to the topography of his travels, suggesting very large and empty spaces; one might think of them as mythological. Indeed the people who populate these landscapes are just that: mythological.

Othello concludes this speech with "This only is the witchcraft I have used" (1.3. 168–170).

Othello's attraction for Desdemona, therefore, along with his personal story of martial adventures, was his craft of storytelling. He opens great imaginative spaces for Desdemona to inhabit with him. The places he refers to are a world apart, a world independent of society, a space without rank, status, prejudice, in some ways a new world.

One phrase, "flood and field," may have inspired Robert Burns to write this ironic stanza about a different kind of warrior:

> I murder hate by flood or field,
> Tho' glory's name may screen us;
> In wars at home I'll spend my blood—
> Life-giving wars of Venus.
> The deities that I adore

Are social Peace and Plenty;
I'm better pleas'd to make one more,
Than be the death of twenty.[75]

7. THE ENDING

The play ends with the deaths of Desdemona and Emilia, both killed by their husbands, for very different reasons.

Emilia is killed by Iago for understanding and revealing the truth. She grasps immediately, as Othello "proves" Desdemona's infidelity, that Iago is to blame. Iago first tells her to keep quiet, but Emilia takes a courageous step and says she would sooner not go home with him again than not speak now: "Perchance, Iago, I will ne'er go home" (5.2.210). Again Iago commands her "hold your peace" (5.2.232), but Emilia refuses: "'Twill out, 'twill out.—I peace? | No, I will speak as liberal as the north"[76] (5.2.232–233). For this, Iago stabs and kills her. Dying, she utters: "So speaking as I think, alas, I die" (5.2.265). Emilia is the only character in the play who fully grasps Iago's treachery. Her last words are ironic. She is honest and fearless.

Othello dies by his own hand, using the sword with which he had fought to maintain order for the Venetian empire. Now he turns it on himself as the only way in which he can hope to serve justice and to return order. Before he kills himself he asks the gathered Venetians to record the true story of Othello—"Set you down this" (5.2.367)—remembering the whole person.

Unusually for Shakespeare's tragedies, the villain, Iago, survives the final scene. Judgement and punishment await him: that is the promise at the end; but it will happen outside the play. This happens in none of the other tragedies examined here.

Cassio is nominated to take Othello's place and govern Cyprus. Cassio was Othello's choice for lieutenant, his second in command in the army. He comes across in the play as a decent man, and he will no doubt take his job seriously.

However, as playgoers in 1603 would be aware, the Ottoman Empire took over Cyprus in 1570, so they would have known that not all was going to be plain sailing for Cassio.

8. CONCLUSIONS: WHAT IS THE TRAGEDY?

We have defined Shakespearean tragedy as the events leading to the undeserved downfall and death of a hero, caused ultimately by a Machiavellian power.

This applies very much to the tragedy *Othello*. Othello is different from Hamlet, in that he is given much space in the play before the seed of his destruction is planted in him. Shakespeare establishes Othello as an honourable, humane, loving person of authority and integrity.

The Machiavellian Iago's true nature is clearly drawn from the start. The audience are made aware of the fact that they can expect evil dealings from him.

There can be no doubt that Iago causes the tragic downfall of Othello, by exploiting his unfamiliarity with Venetian society and its workings. Othello is not used to deception and dishonesty. His values are the opposite: honesty, loyalty, valour. However, these values do not help him when dealing with the Machiavellian force.

We witness the utter destruction of Othello's dignity, his love, his humanity. In cruelly ironic doubling, Othello is driven to destroy Desdemona's happiness and her life when he acts as Iago's extended arm.

By murdering Desdemona, Othello kills something central to himself, the part that made his life worth living. After he arrives in Cyprus he says to Desdemona about their shared love:

> ... If it were now to die,
> 'Twere now to be most happy, for I fear
> My soul hath her content so absolute
> That not another comfort like to this
> Succeeds in unknown fate.
>
> (2.1.192–196)

What makes Othello's downfall so shocking is that we see him unravel before our eyes, and we have Iago informing us of his every destructive and ruthless move.

The audience feel great pity as they experience the undeserved, complete ruination of the heroic Othello, the destruction of his humanity and his love. The killing of Desdemona and Othello are moments of high drama and impart a sense of deep loss and grief to the audience.

FOOTNOTES

58 *Hecatommithi*, similar to Boccaccio's *Decameron*.

59 One famous example of these is Abram Hannibal, kidnapped as a child in Africa and presented to the Russian emperor Peter the Great as a gift, later becoming one of his military leaders. He was the great-grandfather of the Russian poet Alexander Pushkin.

60 meaning ill-fated.

61 Aphrodite, the goddess of love and beauty, was born in Cyprus—an additional irony.

62 See "Note the language" below.

63 Doubling: reinforcing themes through emphasis.

64 Foils: reinforce themes by contrast.

65 To heighten awareness of opposites, the specific nature of one is played off against that of another.

66 This is a device whereby the playwright allows the audience to know more than the characters.

67 Imagery underlines the main themes of a play in a non-verbal manner.

68 A motif in literature is a recurring device that has a symbolic significance and underlines and expands the main themes.

69 Foreshadowing is a kind of dramatic irony where the full truth of a statement becomes apparent only with hindsight.

70 Iambic pentameter is poetry written in lines of ten syllables with five beats. This sounds like a heartbeat or a horse galloping; it is a basic human rhythm: da-DUM da-DUM da-DUM da-DUM da-DUM.

71 We distinguish between metre and rhythm. Metre is the underlying pattern of stressed and unstressed syllables—in Shakespeare mainly (iambic) blank verse. Rhythm is a feature of natural spoken language, which can subtly shift the metre. The interaction between metre and rhythm accentuates the meaning and creates tension in the spoken verse, so that it sounds like natural speech.

72 caves.

73 Greek mythological people-eaters.

74 A mythical race called the Blemmyes.

75 Robert Burns, "I Murder Hate" (song), 1790.

76 Possibly the north wind.

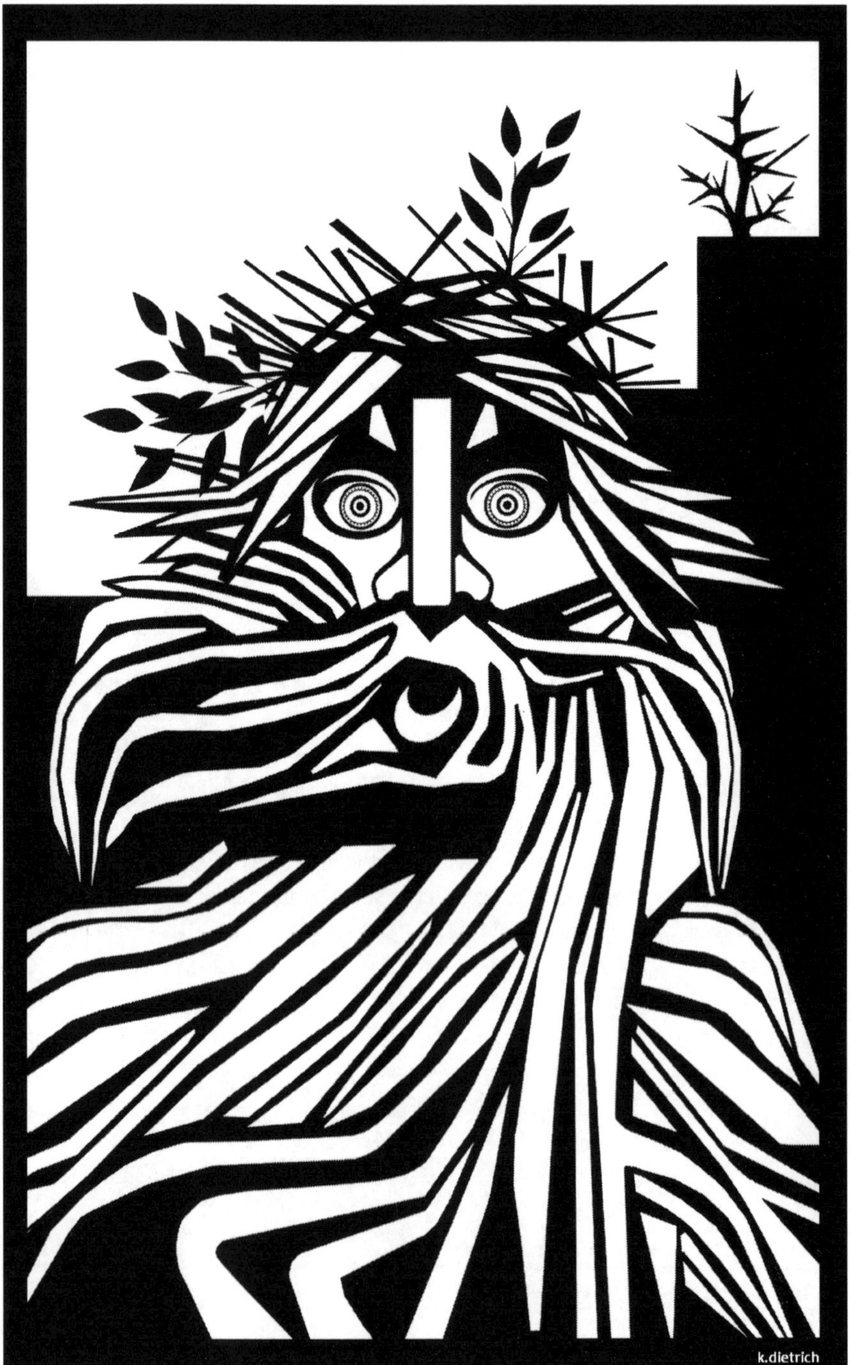
k.dietrich

CHAPTER IV

KING LEAR (1605)

"Reason in madness"
—Act 4, scene 3

While the first two tragedies, *Hamlet* and *Othello*, are set in the not too distant past as far as Shakespeare's contemporaries were concerned, this changes with *King Lear* and *Macbeth*. Both these plays go back to much earlier times in the history of England (*King Lear*) and Scotland (*Macbeth*).

Although all four tragedies in fact explore issues of concern to the Elizabethan or Jacobean playgoer, they are removed either in place (*Hamlet* and *Othello*) or in time (*King Lear* and *Macbeth*). This removal causes a distancing from the events shown on stage; the spectators draw comparisons between these apparently remote events and their own lives and affairs.

King Lear is set in roughly eighth-century England. Shakespeare based his plot on a late sixteenth-century history of Britain, Raphael Holinshed's *Chronicles*, which in turn is based on Geoffrey of Monmouth's twelfth-century *History of the Kings of*

Britain. Holinshed's *Chronicles* were an important source for Shakespeare's history plays and again for *King Lear* and *Macbeth*. However, there were other Elizabethan renderings of this story, most notably in Spenser's *The Faerie Queen*.[77]

1. THE PLOT

The story told in *King Lear* is that of a proud and stubborn eighty-year old king who decides that it is time to retire. He plans to divide his kingdom into three equal parts, one for each of his daughters. However, his vanity leads him to subject them to a "love test," in which they are expected to vie for their share of the kingdom by declaring their devotion to him.

Lear's two elder daughters, Goneril and Regan, have no difficulty in outdoing each other in their insincere flattery. Lear's youngest and favourite daughter, Cordelia, is unable to humour him: she tells him she loves him as she should and when married will share her love between Lear and her husband. Lear is so outraged that he disowns Cordelia and disinherits her. He is particularly offended that she declares that she is telling the truth.

Only one of the courtiers, the Earl of Kent, speaks up for Cordelia. Lear banishes him for this challenge, threatening him with death if he is found in England in six days' time.

Lear insults Cordelia terribly when the King of France asks to marry her, saying that she is worthless. The King of France defends Cordelia's value as being intrinsic to her person, not dependent on a dowry.

Lear decides to stay alternately with Goneril and Regan, for a month at a time. All he requires of them is that an entourage of a hundred knights may stay with him. As the first act closes,

Goneril and Regan discuss how to manage their father, for whom neither has much regard.

In a subplot, the Earl of Gloucester's illegitimate son Edmund persuades his father that his legitimate son, Edgar, is plotting to kill him. Gloucester, outraged, banishes Edgar. Ultimately, Edmund wants the Gloucester title and lands, and he achieves this by first getting rid of Edgar and later betraying Gloucester.

When Lear first stays in Goneril's house she soon tires of his life-style and his hundred knights. She instructs her servants to neglect him openly. He notices their impertinence and has an argument with Goneril, who threatens to reduce the number of knights herself if Lear does not do it. This deep insult causes Lear to leave, hoping for better treatment in Regan's house. Goneril's servant Oswald is despatched with a letter for Regan, to warn her of Lear's arrival.

While Lear is at Goneril's, Kent appears in disguise and enters into Lear's service as "Caius." It emerges later that he had promised Cordelia to stay near the king and protect him. Lear's Fool also enters the play at this stage. Kent and the Fool tell Lear that he has made a great mistake.

Lear sends the disguised Kent ahead with letters for Regan and Gloucester as he prepares to ride to his second daughter's house. Regan and her husband, the Duke of Cornwall, leave their house to avoid Lear and go to Gloucester's, ostensibly to seek his advice on the strife between Lear and Goneril.

Oswald and Kent follow Cornwall and Regan to Gloucester's house to await replies to their letters. Kent picks a fight with Oswald for taking Goneril's side against the king; this results in Cornwall and Regan putting Kent in the stocks—against Gloucester's will, who considers this an insult to Lear. This is exactly the way Lear takes it when he arrives at the scene.

When Regan and Cornwall reluctantly see Lear, Regan demands that he apologise to Goneril, openly taking her sister's side against their father. Together they humiliate Lear by ignoring his wishes and feelings and insisting on an ever greater reduction in the number of his knights, finally denying him any at all.

Lear, at the height of this humiliation, leaves Gloucester's house and goes out onto the heath in a terrible storm with his Fool. Cornwall and Regan, who act as though they, not Gloucester, own the house, lock up the doors and shut Lear out, despite Gloucester's protest.

Kent sends written word regarding the King's situation to Dover, where Cordelia's French troops are expected.

Lear, the Fool and Kent are out on the heath in the storm. Lear's mind becomes unhinged as his world, his values and all he depended on have collapsed. Emptied of these lifelong certainties, his mind goes into a kind of free-fall. But this allows it to grasp previously unacknowledged things and to see matters in a new light. Above all, he comprehends the extent to which he has been deceived and betrayed. In understanding this he gains an insight into his own blindness to other people and their needs, how he has failed his subjects and the poor and has been part of a corrupt system.

Kent brings Lear to a hovel, where they meet Edgar, Gloucester's banished son, disguised as a mad beggar. This group of people, who are all supporters of Lear's and two of whom disguise their identity, form an odd alliance of seemingly mainly mad people in an open space outside noble society. Their space is the territory of the poor, the peasants and beggars, the evicted. This is exactly what Lear, Edgar and Kent now are.

Gloucester, like Kent, is involved in the clandestine conspiracy to help Lear escape by carriage to Dover. He defends Lear to his daughters, courageously accusing Regan to her face of inhuman behaviour. He is punished with horrendous blinding and is banished, stripped of his title and property. So Gloucester too becomes one of the dispossessed. It is Gloucester's servants and tenant peasants who stand by him and take him to the safety of the still-disguised Edgar.

Gloucester, Edgar, Kent and Lear meet again at Dover. Edgar cares for Gloucester and eventually reveals his true identity to his father. Cordelia cares for Lear until both are captured by Edmund, then leader of the English army.

Edgar defeats Edmund in a final combat. Cordelia is put to death. Lear kills the hangman off stage and is saved from hanging because of Edmund's dying change of heart.

Goneril's husband, the Duke of Albany, who after Cornwall's death is *de facto* King of England, returns all power and authority to Lear. Lear dies, and Albany then pronounces Kent and Edgar joint rulers of England. Kent declines, and Edgar vows to rule England in the spirit of Cordelia.

2. WHO ARE THE CHARACTERS?

This play is set in eighth-century England, also called Albion. However, the characters in the play represent the forces in Jacobean society. They are inspired by the old nobility and the younger generation of nobles who are charting their own and different ways forward as early seventeenth-century English society is changing.

The characters are aligned in two groups: those for and those against the tragic hero, Lear.

Lear is a representative of the old feudal nobility. Those who support him do so from a sense of loyalty and honour. Against him are the forces of inhumanity, those more modern, intensely self-interested Machiavellian[78] characters who treat Lear callously, in pursuit of power and their own gain. All Machiavellians are representatives of the younger generation.

However, Shakespeare shows that this generation has also produced people in the tradition of Renaissance humanism, who, like Erasmus's Christian prince,[79] are wise, honest and loyal and have a sense of the common good.

LEAR

Lear is an absolute monarch who has lost touch with his people and with his own understanding. He is free to punish and banish as he thinks fit. He is happy to be flattered and deceived by false professions of affection; indeed he has lost sound political instinct when he decides to divide his kingdom.

His attachment to the hundred knights is a reference to the entourage of the old feudal nobility. Yet he has a system of values whereby he expects decency, respect and loyalty from his children and his courtiers as well as from all his subjects. It does not occur to him that it could be otherwise. His is the strictly ordered feudal world, where a person's place within the hierarchy was clearly defined and could not be changed.

Lear is incapable of understanding the kind of disrespect shown to him by his elder daughters. Their disregard for him and for his dignity once he has handed over his power and his kingdom to them shatters his world utterly. When he abandons the society he has known, and is indeed ejected from it by these daughters, he enters the heath as a naked man, a man who has lost everything.

The tempest that rages on the heath is symbolic of what is going on in Lear's head. In the middle of this violent storm, in the territory of the poor and "mad," Lear gains a profound understanding of the condition of the dispossessed. Before he enters the hovel he prays for "you houseless poverty" (3.4.26)—for the homeless. He realises:

> Poor naked wretches, whereso'er you are,
> That bide the pelting of this pitiless storm,
> How shall your houseless heads and unfed sides,
> Your looped and windowed raggedness, defend you
> From seasons such as these? Oh, I have ta'en
> Too little care of this! Take physic, pomp.
> Expose thyself to feel what wretches feel,
> That thou mayst shake the superflux to them
> And show the heavens more just.
>
> (3.4.28–36)

The shock and the experience of complete dispossession, rejection and ejection are a revelation to Lear. As he is exposed to the poor and the homeless, the evicted, he realises that this is going on in his own kingdom and that he has not taken an interest in the wretched. This insight is not madness but the opposite of madness.

When Lear encounters Edgar, who pretends to be a mad beggar dressed in the most meagre of rags, if not indeed naked, his insight goes further again:

> Why, thou wert better in thy grave than to answer with thy uncovered body this extremity of the skies.—Is man

no more than this? Consider him well.—Thou owest the worm no silk, the beast no hide, the sheep no wool, the cat no perfume. Ha! Here's three on's are sophisticated. Thou art the thing itself. Unaccommodated man is no more but such a poor, bare, forked animal as thou art.—Off, off, you lendings! Come. Unbutton here. (tears at his clothes)

(3.4.93–102)

Lear discovers an essential commonness between the mad beggar and himself and illustrates this in their nakedness—quite literally, stripped of everything. Here he discovers essential humanity, "the thing itself," "unaccommodated man." This is a crucial moment in Lear's development. Symbolically, to emphasise this new understanding he tears off his clothes.

Of course there are also expressions of genuine madness, sometimes simply for comic relief; but very often there is hidden reason in these, such as in Lear's mock trial of Goneril and Regan, with Edgar and the Fool as judges. He asks:

> Then let them anatomise Regan. See what breeds about her heart. Is there any cause in nature that makes these hard hearts?
>
> (3.6.70–73)

This mock trial is an inversion of the play's opening "love test." Instead of expecting superficial flattery, Lear here seeks a scientific, objective examination of what makes hard hearts. He has come a long way.

Later in the play, when Lear meets the blinded Gloucester near Dover, he continues to be "unhinged," asking questions relating to social injustice, such as:

> A man may see how this world goes with no eyes. Look with thine ears. See how yon justice rails upon yon simple thief. Hark in thine ear: change places and, handy-dandy, which is the justice, which is the thief?
> (4.6.140–143)

Or he comments:

> Through tattered clothes great vices do appear;
> Robes and furred gowns hide all. Plate sin with gold,
> And the strong lance of justice hurtless breaks.
> Arm it in rags, a pigmy's straw does pierce it.
> (4.6.152–155)

Edgar too recognises Lear's deep new understanding, commenting: "Reason in madness" (4.6.162–163). This is a profound growth in humanity in Lear. Had Lear simply been turned out onto the heath, railing against his humiliation, and died, the play would be sad and would no doubt generate sympathy with him. However, Lear's destruction means the loss of his new understanding of the plight of the dispossessed, his appreciation of the fundamental equality of human beings, the loss of his new humanity. This makes his death tragic.

GLOUCESTER

Gloucester is a parallel character to Lear. He is the father figure in the subplot.

Gloucester, like Lear, is gullible at the beginning of the play, believing all too easily Edmund's lies about Edgar, banishing and disinheriting him. Gloucester is also superstitious, something the younger generation are definitely not. He questions Lear's wisdom in abdicating power, yet he is happy to attribute the old values going awry to "These late eclipses in the sun and moon" (1.2.98).

He shares with Lear the sense of respect and loyalty due to a king and a parent, and they have the same values regarding hospitality and basic decency. Gloucester stands up against the humiliation of Lear by Cornwall and Regan in his own house. He is very unhappy about Kent being put in the stocks, and tries to prevent Lear's eviction from his house. Gloucester thus becomes the victim of the most heinous act of violence in the play, his blinding by Cornwall—again, in his own house.

His loyalty to Lear, and his having the courage of his convictions, align him with Kent, who challenges Lear's treatment of Cordelia and who, despite his banishment, stays with Lear in disguise throughout the play. Gloucester, like Kent, is party to the clandestine plan to rescue Lear and bring him to his allies at Dover.

Gloucester's failure is his inability to see through Edmund, to truly understand his new, Machiavellian values. Gloucester, like Lear, is thrown out onto the heath, stripped of his title and properties.

It is here that Gloucester too treats the poor like fellow human beings. After his blinding he is first taken care of by his servants. They take him to a peasant who has rented Gloucester's land for generations. When he is handed over to Edgar, disguised as a beggar, Gloucester asks the peasant for clothes for this poor madman: "bring some covering for this naked soul." The peasant promises to "bring him the best 'parel that I have" (4.1.46, 51). This short utterance, the only one where the poor actually speak in this play, is a statement of dignity and generosity to a fellow-human.

Just like Lear, Gloucester arrives at an insight into human equality on the heath: "I' th' last night's storm I such a fellow saw, | Which made me think a man a worm . . . | As flies to wanton boys are we to th' gods. | They kill us for their sport" (4.1.35–40). And his insight into social corruption and the indifference of the powerful towards the poor also parallels that of Lear:

> Let the superfluous and lust-dieted man,
> That slaves your ordinance, that will not see
> Because he doth not feel, feel your power quickly.
> So distribution should undo excess,
> And each man have enough.
> (4.1.68–172)

This dramatic doubling, the fact that both men, Gloucester and Lear, arrive at a very similar understanding of social injustice and a basic equality of all humankind, underlines and heightens the importance attributed to this insight by Shakespeare.

These are not the laughable ravings of a madman: this is the consequence when one puts oneself into the position of the impoverished and powerless and sees the world from their viewpoint. Both of them believe that such identification with the dispossessed would lead to a fairer distribution of wealth. In the case of Lear and Gloucester they arrive at such an understanding when they are "mad" and blind and stripped of everything, when they have found themselves in the place of the wretched.

CORDELIA

Cordelia possesses the qualities of Erasmus's Christian prince. She is the honest and wise humanist who will "follow the right, do violence to no one, plunder no one, sell no public office, be corrupted by no bribes."[80] She is established as an independent, loyal character, willing to sacrifice her life for justice.

Cordelia is on stage only in act 1, scene 1, and then again at the end of the play. For most of the action she is off stage, acting on behalf of Lear and England. As she disappears after the opening scene for much of the play, it is dramatically important to give the audience a sense of her moral strength. Here Cordelia is introduced as honest and unafraid:

> I yet beseech your majesty,
> If for I want that glib and oily art
> To speak and purpose not—since what I well intend,
> I'll do 't before I speak—that you make known
> It is no vicious blot, murder, or foulness,
> No unchaste action or dishonoured step
> That hath deprived me of your grace and favour
>
> (1.1.224–230)

Cordelia is banished from the court, disinherited and shamed by a foolish father. The King of France takes her as his wife. He also possesses the understanding and qualities of a humanist, a Christian prince, and is a true partner to her. She wins the sympathy and loyalty of the spectators, who see Lear, Goneril and Regan for what they are at the beginning of the play.

Cordelia is also the parallel character to Gloucester's Edgar.

She, like Edgar, is wronged. She, like Edgar, loves and protects her father. Earlier than Edgar, she has the wisdom to know who the enemy is, and she will do something about it: she raises an army to revert England to Lear.

When Cordelia returns to England with the French army, in act 4, scene 4, she orders her people to seek out and help her father and consults a doctor on his treatment. Her virtue and devotion are manifest in her willingness to forgive her father for his awful behaviour. At one point she declares, "O dear father, | It is thy business that I go about" (4.4.23–24), echoing a biblical passage in which Christ says, "I must go about my father's business" (Luke 2:49).

When Lear finally reunites with Cordelia he expresses humility and repentance: "I am a very foolish fond old man" (4.7.58), he tells her sadly, and he admits that she has "some cause" to hate him (4.7.73). Cordelia's moving response, "No cause, no cause" (4.7.74), seals their reconciliation.

Love and forgiveness, embodied in Lear's best daughter, join with humility and repentance, and for a brief time happiness prevails. Although Cordelia dies as a result of Edmund's machinations, Edgar, who is proclaimed king by Albany, vows to rule in her spirit.

EDGAR

Edgar is Lear's godson. He is Gloucester's legitimate son, and thereby a contrast to the illegitimate Edmund is established. In a soliloquy, Edmund confirms that Edgar is his greatest obstacle and therefore his enemy.

Edmund engineers a situation in which he makes Gloucester believe that Edgar is plotting against him; and when the unsuspecting Edgar appears, Edmund further incriminates him. Unlike Cordelia, Edgar is at first fooled by his Machiavellian sibling.

Edgar is disinherited and banished, indeed condemned to death by Gloucester, without seeking any verification of Edmund's claim:

> Not in this land shall he remain uncaught.
> And found—dispatch . . .
> . . . I will proclaim it
> That he which finds him shall deserve our thanks,
> Bringing the murderous coward to the stake.
> He that conceals him, death.
>
> (2.1.58–64)

The last two lines here are chilling indeed. The person who finds and delivers Edgar will be rewarded, and Edgar will be burnt at the stake; anybody found to be hiding Edgar will receive the death penalty.

Edgar enters the play more fully in act 3, scene 4, when he is in the hovel on the heath and all but unclothed. He pretends to be mad and calls himself "Poor Tom."[81]

Edgar convinces those he meets on the heath of his madness, although he does not just talk complete nonsense. However, it appears so to Lear and the others, as he speaks of being persecuted by the Devil and about the rottenness of society: "Do Poor Tom some charity, whom the foul | fiend vexes" (3.4.56–57).

When Lear asks him who he had been, he answers:

> A servingman . . . I spake words and broke them in the sweet face of heaven . . . False of heart, light of ear,

bloody of hand—hog in sloth, fox in stealth, wolf in greediness, dog in madness, lion in prey.
(3.4.78–86)

Edgar, like Lear and Gloucester, has arrived at an understanding of corruption and injustice as a result of his eviction from society and his ensuing impoverishment.

When Gloucester enters the hovel and tells Lear, "Our flesh and blood, my lord, is grown so vile | That it doth hate what gets it," Edgar reacts: "Poor Tom's a-cold" (3.4.133–135), showing how upset he is to hear that his father thinks he hates him. Yet he does not reveal his identity; in fact when Lear asks him, "What is your study," he replies, again not untruthfully, "How to prevent the fiend and to kill vermin" (3.4.146–147). This is exactly what Edgar has set out to do, and ultimately what he achieves.

In Lear's mock trial he appoints Edgar the judge. Lear's high emotions during this trial move Edgar to tears: "My tears begin to take his part so much, | They'll mar my counterfeiting" (3.6.56–57). At the end of this scene, in a soliloquy, Edgar promises he will reveal his identity when he has been proved innocent:

... thyself bewray
When false opinion, whose wrong thought defiles thee,
In thy just proof repeals and reconciles thee.
(3.6.106–108)

When Gloucester is blinded by Cornwall he unsuspectingly calls for Edmund, whereupon Regan tells him, "Thou call'st on him that hates thee" (3.7.88). Ironically, Gloucester suddenly sees the truth: "O my follies! Then Edgar was abused" (3.7.91).

And as he is cast out onto the heath again, Edgar leads him to Dover, caring for him and treating him with great gentleness, although withholding his true identity until the very end.

When Edgar challenges Edmund at the end of the play, this is more than personal revenge: it is a battle between the humanism he represents and Edmund's Machiavellian inhumanity. Before they draw swords, Edgar condemns Edmund: "thou art a traitor, | False to thy gods, thy brother, and thy father, | Conspirant 'gainst this high illustrious prince" (5.3.137–139). This is the climax of the play, which fittingly ends with the choice of Edgar as the new king. Edgar accepts this title, promising to rule England as Cordelia could have: "The weight of this sad time we must obey. | Speak what we feel, not what we ought to say" (5.3.334–335).

GONERIL AND REGAN

Goneril and Regan (and Cornwall) are the self-interested younger-generation Machiavellians in this play, along with Edmund. It is clear to the audience from the start that they are adept at deception. However, just how inhuman they are is revealed only in their actions over time. In many ways they seem quite modern to us in their thinking and acting. Genuine affection, honesty and loyalty mean nothing to them; personal gain is everything, even if it costs the dignity and life of others.

When Lear first goes to stay with Goneril soon after the love test and the division of his kingdom, she tells her servants to neglect Lear in her house:

Put on what weary negligence you please,

> You and your fellow servants. I'll have it come to question.
> If he distaste it, let him to our sister,
> Whose mind and mine I know in that are one,
> Not to be overruled.
>
> (1.3.12–16)

Together, Goneril and Regan deprive Lear of his dignity when they tell him he cannot keep his entourage:

> Goneril: What need you five and twenty, ten, or five
> To follow in a house where twice so many
> Have a command to tend you?
> Regan: What need one?
>
> (2.4.252–254)

Often it is Regan who makes a bad punishment worse. When Cornwall puts Kent in the stocks she urges him to leave him there longer, and longer again: "Till noon? Till night, my lord, and all night too" (2.2.125).

And as Lear, bitterly hurt, leaves Gloucester's castle, heading into the storm, Goneril counsels Cornwall to let him go:

> My lord, entreat him by no means to stay.
>
> (2.4.290)

Again, Regan is harsher:

> ... Shut up your doors.
> He is attended with a desperate train.
> And what they may incense him to, being apt

> To have his ear abused, wisdom bids fear.
>
> (2.4.295–298)

Both Goneril and Regan are ready not only to support killers but to kill themselves. This is how the malicious blinding of Gloucester in his own house comes about. Regan tells Cornwall: "Hang him instantly" and Goneril advises: "Pluck out his eyes" (3.7.4). Cornwall acts on Goneril's suggestion. Regan urges her husband to tie Gloucester down more tightly and to blind him in both eyes. She also knifes a servant to death who comes to the defence of Gloucester at the time of his blinding: "Give me thy sword.—A peasant stand up thus" (3.7. 80). At this point Regan proves herself to be worse than Lady Macbeth, who, while she supports her husband in his killings, never kills anybody herself. Here Shakespeare goes further than in any of the other tragedies, in that he shows these two women to be willing murderers.

It is Goneril who poisons Regan at the end of the play and then takes her own life violently by stabbing herself in the heart.

The fact that Edmund is their closest ally in their Machiavellian nature is underlined by Shakespeare, in that they vie for his favour. Not one of these characters has any regard for any other human being besides themselves. Edmund is quite realistic about them and is equally callous.

EDMUND

Edmund, together with Iago in Othello, is the most clearly villainous character in the four tragedies right from the start. Both are, to early seventeenth-century playgoers, the most obviously indebted to the Vice character of the morality plays, the irredeemable personification of evil.

He is introduced at the very beginning of the play by his father, Gloucester, as his illegitimate son. Although he has been acknowledged and looked after by his natural father, Edmund feels he is losing out in his rightful inheritance: "Well then, | Legitimate Edgar, I must have your land" (1.2.15–16).

Edmund devises a situation in which he makes Gloucester believe that Edgar is plotting against him by giving him a letter apparently written by Edgar, which gives voice to Edmund's own belief: "This policy and reverence of age makes the world bitter to the best of our times, keeps our fortunes from us" (1.2.45–47).

Edmund further incriminates Edgar and pretends to have been wounded in a sword fight with him. The result is that Gloucester banishes Edgar.

So Edmund has achieved one of his ends, the disinheritance and banishing of Edgar. Gloucester proclaims that he will make Edmund his heir: "And of my land, | Loyal and natural boy, I'll work the means | To make thee capable" (2.1.84–86). Edmund has brought about all by lies, insinuation, and deception.

Edmund is resolved to gain his inheritance sooner rather than later; now it is Gloucester who stands in the way and needs to be removed. Edmund's chance arises when Gloucester unsuspectingly tells him of a letter describing the French invasion of England in defence of Lear's interests. This is Edmund's opportunity: he will betray Gloucester.

> This ... must draw me
> That which my father loses—no less than all.
> The younger rises when the old doth fall.
>
> (3.3.20–22)

Edmund realises that he will get rid of Gloucester for ever that way, as Cornwall and the English side will consider support for Lear high treason. Cornwall rewards Edmund, making him Earl of Gloucester (3.5.15) and telling him: "I will lay trust upon thee, and thou shalt find a dearer father in my love" (3.5.22–23).

Two scenes later, Gloucester is brought before Cornwall and sentenced without trial. Edmund is sent away by Cornwall, to spare him witnessing the punishment he has caused: "Farewell, my lord of Gloucester" (3.7.11).

At this point Edmund has not yet reached the pinnacle of his ambition. To marry either Regan or Goneril would elevate him even more: he would be regent. He woos both of them, and they fight over him.

Cornwall has died in the aftermath of Gloucester's blinding, and Albany is extremely disenchanted with Goneril and in support of Lear. Edmund concludes: "To both these sisters have I sworn my love . . . Neither can be enjoyed | If both remain alive" (5.1.58–62). Clearly, Edmund would be happy to see either sister dead. In the same soliloquy he admits to hoping to have Albany killed as well as Lear and Cordelia. Edmund intends to walk over many dead bodies in his desire to be king.

The climax of the play is the combat between Edgar and Edmund. Edmund admits to his evil machinations before dying: "What you have charged me with, that have I done— | And more, much more. The time will bring it out" (5.3.168–169). As he dies, so do Regan and Goneril: "I was contracted to them both. All three | Now marry in an instant" (5.3.236–237).

Edmund suffers some remorse in the end. "I pant for life. Some good I mean to do | Despite of mine own nature" (5.3.251–252), and he tries to save the lives of Lear and Cordelia. It comes too late for Cordelia, and Lear dies in grief.

In the character of Edmund, Shakespeare etches the clearest, most ruthless of Machiavellians in this play. Edmund pursues his aim from the very beginning of the play and has no redeeming qualities.

THE FOOL

The Fool is a different kind of character in the play. He is a legacy from the popular theatre tradition of the travelling players. Fools, clowns and court jesters had a licence to tell truths in a witty way. The Fool is the character in the play who we can rely on not to deceive, who can openly tell the truth, no matter what.

In this play he is the only character who can openly criticise Lear without fear of banishment or death. He is a voice of reason and can mock Lear rather than flatter him.

The Fool is immediately on the side of Kent and Cordelia, indeed comes forth only reluctantly after Cordelia's departure. Despite his criticism of Lear's great foolishness, he is loyal to the king and never leaves his side. He accompanies him from his own house to Goneril's and then on to Gloucester's, from where he goes out onto the heath with Lear.

The Fool is present until Lear is sent secretly by carriage to Dover; and Kent enlists his help in taking charge of Lear: "Come, help to bear thy master. | Thou must not stay behind" (3.6.95–96). The Fool disappears from the play at this point.

The Fool has insights into a corrupt society that underline those of Lear and Gloucester. His prophecy at the end of act 3, scene 2, moves from describing a corrupt society to envisaging a utopian one:

> This is a brave night to cool a courtesan.
> I'll speak a prophecy ere I go.
> When priests are more in word than matter,
> When brewers mar their malt with water,
> When nobles are their tailors' tutors,
> No heretics burned but wenches' suitors,
> When every case in law is right,
> No squire in debt nor no poor knight,
> When slanders do not live in tongues,
> Nor cutpurses come not to throngs,
> When usurers tell their gold i' th' field,
> And bawds and whores do churches build—
> Then shall the realm of Albion
> Come to great confusion.
> Then comes the time, who lives to see 't,
> That going shall be used with feet.
>
> (3.2.76–91)

The prophecy falls into two parts. The first two lines refer to corrupt Elizabethan society, where priests speak in a more holy way than they act, and brewers dilute their beer with water.

Then our expectation is undermined. While the first two things might seem commonplace, how likely is it that noblemen would teach their tailors to sew? There is a further shift in the next line, which refers to a practice in Shakespeare's time, the burning at the stake of heretics. Instead of heretics, the Fool suggests, lovers should be "burned" by syphilis.

Following this further shift in an upside-down world, the remaining six lines outline a perfect, utopian world, where there is justice, no poverty, no slander, no thieving, where moneylenders leave cities, and the excommunicated (socially most despised?) build churches. England will then be different from the way it is now: it will be in confusion, but it will be the way it should be, and not upside-down: "Going shall be used with feet."

The logic of the Fool's prophecy is similar to the insights gained and the social comments made by Edgar, Lear and Gloucester at different times on the heath. These four characters on the one hand criticise the corruption and injustice of the society that has ejected them and on the other hand also define a better world.

The Fool is not considered a character in quite the same way as the other figures in the play. He is less complex and psychologically drawn; he both reaches into the popular clown tradition and performs a commenting role, in some ways as revealing as imagery. What is important for us is that he is never deceptive; he may speak in riddles at times, but he always tells the truth.

3. WHAT IS THE PLAY ABOUT?

THE THREAT OF A NEW MACHIAVELLIAN ORDER

A major theme in this play is the cataclysmic clash of social orders: the old absolute, feudal monarch is deprived of his royal status and power, his dignity, his right to house and home, by his elder daughters, the new Machiavellian generation.

Plot and characters in this play show that the old feudal order is not equipped to deal with this new force. Their main representative, Lear, is foolish, vain and superstitious at the beginning of the play, when he relinquishes his power to his elder daughters.

Gloucester doubles Lear in many respects but also displays characteristics worth preserving: a sense of loyalty and honesty. Both he and Kent, who is neither foolish nor superstitious, defend Lear courageously.

So, Shakespeare draws a differentiated picture of the old order: the baby is not thrown out with the bath water. He shows that new social formations grow out of preceding ones, and that the positive aspects of the old should be retained.

Equally, alongside the dangerous, indeed murderous new power there are humanist forces that are in a position to lead society forward in an inclusive, honest and humane way. In this play they are found in the characters of Cordelia and Edgar.

GOOD KINGSHIP OR LEADERSHIP

In this play, as in *Hamlet* and *Macbeth*, Shakespeare brings to the fore the question of what makes a good leader, or king.

Such leaders must be, above all, honest and wise and must act in the interests of the common good. They must not be self-interested. Edgar fully achieves this only after he is exposed to the suffering on the heath, after witnessing and experiencing what the disempowered and dispossessed feel.

Good leaders must be willing to sacrifice their lives in the defeat of evil forces, as both Cordelia and Edgar do.

THE FUNDAMENTAL EQUALITY OF HUMANKIND

Lear, the anointed king, is driven into a space outside this new society. At that moment he shares his life with the naked wretches of his realm, recognises and affirms their common humanity. Lear discovers human dignity in the lowest: the evicted, the "Poor naked wretches," the "houseless heads and unfed sides." Humanity is "the thing itself," "Unaccommodated man," "a poor, bare, forked animal," and Lear finds this in a situation of humiliation, subjugation, desolation, and contempt.

As Lear takes leave of his feudal understanding of social hierarchy he intuitively understands his commonality with those of his subjects who have nothing. This in turn makes him realise the enormous social inequity and corruption in his kingdom, wrongs for which he is responsible. Ultimately his experience leads him to understand that only a fair distribution of wealth can remedy this.

SOCIAL INJUSTICE CREATED BY SOCIAL HIERARCHY

All the outcasts on the heath arrive at an understanding that the way things are in England is wrong. All of them describe corruption, the ignorance of the powerful, and the indifference towards the poor. They all envisage the possibility of a different kind of society, one in which, as the Fool says, the world will be put on its feet. This theme of a utopia, of what might be, is inherent in the central themes of the play.

4. THE DRAMA OF IT ALL

Studying Shakespeare's plays is a very rewarding experience in many ways. One of these is seeing just how he creates the drama. Shakespeare uses a variety of dramatic devices to heighten the theatrical experience. Among these are:

DOUBLING[82]

• Gloucester and Lear, Cordelia and Edgar, Edmund and Goneril-Regan-Cornwall all double each other. What these pairs have in common emphasises the point Shakespeare is making about them. Nothing happens by chance.

CONTRAST[83]

• The Machiavellian v. the old nobility v. the humanist.
• Lear's love trial v. the imagined trial of Goneril and Regan on the heath.
• The sequencing of scenes, to contrast different forces or atmospheres. For example, events before Gloucester's castle in act 2 are interrupted by a short scene (act 2, scene 3) of Edgar in the woods, who explains how he will disguise himself to escape without trace. Also, the scenes on the heath are alternated with scenes in and around Gloucester's castle.

DRAMATIC IRONY[84]

• This is often found in soliloquies or asides, where a character reveals inner thoughts to the spectators, often making them aware of things that the characters in the play are not aware of. For example, Edmund makes known in a soliloquy how he is going to get rid of Edgar and voices his ultimate aim of taking Gloucester's title.
• It can be situational irony, the appearance of characters in unexpected situations: for example, Edgar appears in the middle of Edmund's revelation of his plans.
• It can also manifest itself as verbal irony, where the playwright

knows the future of a character and situation that the characters themselves and the audience are unaware of, for example Kent's comment about Edmund being a decent person in the opening minutes of the play: "I cannot wish the fault undone, the issue of it being so proper" (1.1.16–17); or when Lear says to Regan about Goneril, "Her eyes are fierce, but thine | Do comfort and not burn" (2.4.161–162).

IMAGERY[85]

- For instance, the crown that Lear never wears (it is carried before him leading up to the love test) until he is spotted with a crown of weeds near Dover. Also the Fool, referring to the foolishness of splitting the crown in two, giving it away to Cornwall and Albany, compares this to a broken eggshell and even refers to Lear's head as a bald crown: "Thou hadst little wit in thy bald crown when thou gavest thy golden one away" (1.4.145–146).
- The storm is an image for the collapse of the ordered world that Lear thought he had inhabited and his mental upheaval.
- Sight and blindness (metaphorical and actual): There are many references to eyes. They begin with Goneril's assertion that her love for Lear is "Dearer than eyesight" (1.1.55). Then there is Gloucester's blinding, the idea of which is brought about by his defence of Lear to Regan: "Because I would not see thy cruèl nails | Pluck out his poor old eyes" (3.7.54–55). It is shockingly ironic that he becomes "seeing" at the moment of his blindness. This is emphasised when Lear tells the blind Gloucester: "A man may see how this world goes with no eyes. Look with thine ears" (4.6.140–141).
- Clothing is an important image. Edgar disguises himself as a

practically naked, mad beggar; later he is given Gloucester's tenant's best peasant clothes; and later again he appears in armour as he battles with Edmund and reveals his identity. Kent too takes on the disguise of a poor man, as he is forced to adopt a different identity in order to stay close to Lear.
- Lear's nakedness expresses directly and vividly his understanding of the commonality of humankind. In nakedness he recognises essential human equality, "the thing itself" (3.4.98).
- Animal imagery: Goneril and Regan are equated with predators by Gloucester: "thy fierce sister | In his anointed flesh stick boarish fangs" (3.7.55–56). Lear speaking to Goneril: "thy wolvish visage" (1.4.297); and Albany articulates: "Tigers, not daughters" (4.2.39).
- There is also Lear's identification and comradeship "with the wolf and owl" (2.4.199).
- Lear further uses animal imagery when referring to corrupt society: "There thou mightst behold the great image of authority: a dog's obeyed in office" (4.6.146–147).

MOTIF [86]

- Madness: Edgar's feigned madness is part of his disguise but also allows him to articulate insights. Lear's "madness" is a manifestation of a total loss of all certainties.

FORESHADOWING [87]

- Lear's banishment of Cordelia foreshadows his own eviction by his other daughters.
- When Lear first appears in the play, the stage direction reads: "Enter one bearing a coronet" (1.1.31). Lear does not wear the

crown, nor will he again.
- From the beginning there are many references to eyesight, which is important throughout the play in the form of metaphorical and actual blindness. (See Imagery above.)
- The repetition of "Nothing" (1.1.86–89) in the exchange between Cordelia and Lear during the love test foreshadows the importance of Nothing as Lear loses all and ends up with nothing on the heath. "Nothing" is echoed in nakedness.

5. CLOSE FOCUS: THE MACHIAVELLIAN'S CREDO

ACT 1, SCENE 2

This is the scene where Edmund reveals himself as a villain when he manipulates his father, Gloucester, into thinking that Edgar is plotting an intrigue against him.

The scene is full of dramatic devices that heighten the tension and thereby the audience's enjoyment of the play. They include the use of soliloquy as a means of dramatic irony, the clever use of language in insinuation, foreshadowing, comic relief, and situational irony.

Edmund has a soliloquy at the beginning, in the middle and at the end of the scene. This scene fully establishes the character of Edmund, and he dominates it. He appears as the puppet-master as he pulls the strings and manipulates both Gloucester and Edgar in front of the spectators' eyes.

Apart from a brief introduction to Kent in act 1, scene 1, this is Edmund's first appearance. In his first soliloquy Edmund reveals his innermost thoughts to himself and so to the audience. This is his opening statement about himself. He declares how he feels, deprived of his inheritance because of his illegitimacy, and what he proposes to do to change this:

> Well, my legitimate, if this letter speed
> And my invention thrive, Edmund the base
> Shall top th' legitimate. I grow, I prosper.
> Now, gods, stand up for bastards!
>
> (19–22)

He reveals his plans quite openly. This is rather horrifying for the spectators. They are now aware of Edmund's plans and know more than the other characters in the play. Such dramatic irony creates tension, as the audience can see characters fall into traps set by Edmund.

As Gloucester walks in on Edmund, he comments on the foolishness of Lear:

> Kent banished thus? And France in choler parted?
> And the king gone tonight, prescribed his power
> Confined to exhibition? All this done
> Upon the gad?
>
> (23–26)

And Shakespeare loses no time. Edmund begins his intrigue right away, and Gloucester immediately steps into the same trap as Lear, of believing the dishonest child. At this point the doubling of Lear and Gloucester is established.

Edmund operates his intrigue largely by means of suggestion and deception. In this scene, insinuation is very dramatic in its effect on Gloucester:

> I beseech you, sir, pardon me. It is a letter from my

> brother that I have not all o'er-read. And for so much as I have perused, I find it not fit for your o'erlooking.
>
> (36–38)

This is only one instance of many where tension mounts as Gloucester is further and further lured into believing Edmund's lies. Edmund's apparent attempts at restraining Gloucester's rage cleverly manipulate Gloucester into believing that Edmund is trustworthy. The audience would find this both funny and terrifying.

Before Gloucester leaves the scene he unknowingly foreshadows what will happen in the course of the play:

> Love cools, friendship falls off, brothers divide, in cities mutinies, in countries discord, in palaces treason, and the bond cracked 'twixt son and father . . . Machinations, hollowness, treachery, and all ruinous disorders follow us disquietly to our graves.
>
> (101–108)

Gloucester's exit gives rise to Edmund's second soliloquy. In it he laughs at Gloucester's superstitions, and he confirms his awareness of his base nature. Ironically, just as Edmund mentions Edgar's name, Edgar walks in—onto the stage. Edmund comments on this irony:

> . . . and pat on's cue he comes like the catastrophe of the old comedy. My cue is villainous melancholy, with a sigh like Tom o' Bedlam. Oh, these eclipses do portend these divisions! fa, sol, la, mi.
>
> (126–129)

This is intentionally funny. Edmund is having a laugh with the spectators; he is comparing Edgar to the Catastrophe character of the popular theatre, while he compares himself to "villainous melancholy," another character. At the same time, more sinisterly, he foreshadows the disguise soon to be adopted by Edgar, that of Tom o' Bedlam. He also has a laugh at his father's superstition. This complicity with the audience is possible only in the theatre.

Edmund's insinuations are now worked on Edgar; so there is more doubling, Edgar's gullibility matching that of Gloucester. Again, Edmund succeeds in his deception and gets Edgar to engage in them unwittingly. It is, of course, ironic that Edgar should comment to Edmund: "Some villain hath done me wrong" (154); and Edmund replies to this: "That's my fear" (155).

When Edgar leaves shortly after this, Edmund concludes at the end of the scene:

> A credulous father, and a brother noble—
> Whose nature is so far from doing harms
> That he suspects none
>
> (167–169)

Edmund has controlled this scene completely. This is his scene. We learn everything about him, his controlling and manipulative nature, and about what he is planning to do. From now on, through this dramatic irony, the spectator knows more than the characters and can watch the drama unfold in all its horror.

6. NOTE THE LANGUAGE

As in all his plays, in *King Lear* Shakespeare mainly uses blank verse in iambic pentameter,[88] and prose. Blank verse is usually reserved for the speech of the nobility. In this example Lear is cursing Goneril[89]:

> You nimble lightnings, dart your blinding flames
> Into her scornful eyes! Infect her beauty,
> You fen-sucked fogs drawn by the powerful sun,
> To fall and blister! (2.4.154–157)

Prose is typically used for characters of a lower class or indeed for the mad. In *King Lear*, Edgar and Lear speak in prose when feigning madness or actually mad. Lear, speaking at the mock trial, says:

> Then let them anatomize Regan. See what breeds about her heart. Is there any cause in nature that makes these hard hearts? (to Edgar) You, sir, I entertain you for one of my hundred. Only I do not like the fashion of your garments. You will say they are Persian attire, but let them be changed.
> (3.6.70–75)

Or Edgar:

> The foul fiend haunts Poor Tom in the voice of a nightingale. Hoppedance cries in Tom's belly for two white herring. Croak not, black angel. I have no food for thee.
> (3.6.27–29)

Edgar and the Fool also use other variations of verse. When Edgar resumes his noble identity he returns to speaking in blank verse.

THE BEAUTY OF THE LANGUAGE

Here is a wonderful example of word painting. Edgar describes to Gloucester what he sees at the bottom of the imaginary cliff he has brought him to in act 4, scene 6:

> Come on, sir. Here's the place. Stand still. How fearful
> And dizzy 'tis to cast one's eyes so low!
> The crows and choughs that wing the midway air
> Show scarce so gross as beetles. Half way down
> Hangs one that gathers samphire—dreadful trade!
> Methinks he seems no bigger than his head.
> The fishermen that walk upon the beach
> Appear like mice. And yon tall anchoring bark,
> Diminished to her cock, her cock a buoy
> Almost too small for sight. The murmuring surge
> That on th' unnumbered idle pebbles chafes
> Cannot be heard so high. I'll look no more
> Lest my brain turn and the deficient sight
> Topple down headlong.
>
> (4.6.11–24)

These lines conjure up a vivid scene, full of movement, sound and sights on the cliff, on the beach, in mid-air, and on the sea; it is an all-encompassing image of outdoor life, a finely woven fabric of human and natural existence. It is reminiscent of Achilles' shield, as described by Homer.[90] It is poignant that

Edgar describes for a suicidal Gloucester such a happy and purposeful image of life.

7. THE ENDING

In this tragedy the tragic hero, Lear, and his fellow-hero, Gloucester, both die. Neither of them dies violently, although they have suffered much violence. Both die of a broken heart, of enormous fatigue following their suffering. Both have lost and regained children, both have been betrayed and been treated viciously by their Machiavellian offspring and then felt redeemed by the humanist daughter or son they rejected. They are not physically destroyed, as Hamlet, Othello and Macbeth are.

In this tragedy the Machiavellians are destroyed—each and every one of them: Edmund is defeated by Edgar, Cornwall dies of wounds inflicted by a servant of Gloucester's after his blinding, and Goneril poisons Regan and then kills herself.

Only Cordelia is hanged, by order of Edmund; so she dies by the extended arm of the Machiavellian. Edgar is the avenger; he is made king. Edgar, who has suffered with Lear and Gloucester and has achieved the same insights, will preserve their humanity and put it to use in his kingship. His promise is to reign in the spirit of Cordelia.

8. CONCLUSIONS: WHAT IS THE TRAGEDY?

We have defined Shakespearean tragedy as the events leading to the undeserved downfall and death of a hero, caused ultimately by a Machiavellian power. The tragedy is the destruction of the humane core of the tragic hero. This is what evokes our compassion and grief.

Lear is introduced at the beginning of the play as a foolish, vain absolute monarch. He is easily deceived by his Machiavellian daughters into believing they love him more than themselves. He blindly rejects Cordelia, whom he banishes and disinherits.

When these elder daughters mirror his treatment of Cordelia by banishing Lear and stripping him of all he has, his mind becomes unhinged as he is evicted and driven to the heath.

At this point, when he reaches the very bottom, Lear discovers human dignity. He finds it as an outcast, among those who have been humiliated, subjugated, scorned, and abandoned. This humanises Lear. He reaches insights into the corruption of his society and the abject nakedness of the poor, with whom he is now equal, with whom he identifies and sympathises.

This enormous growth in humanity, which is doubled by Gloucester, caused by an exposure to feeling with the wretches, defines the tragedy and means that Lear has indeed been "more sinned against than sinning" (3.2.58). His unparalleled insight is destroyed with his death.

FOOTNOTES

77 Book II, Canto X.
78 A Machiavellian is a ruthless, unprincipled egotist in pursuit of power, wealth, and status. He is willing to use any kind of deceit to achieve his aims and does not shrink from murder. See chapter I above, "The context, humanism, and Machiavellianism."
79 Desiderius Erasmus, *The Education of a Christian Prince*, chapter I, "The qualities, education, and significance of a Christian prince."
80 Desiderius Erasmus, *The Education of a Christian Prince*, chapter I, "The qualities, education, and significance of a Christian prince."
81 The reason for this particular guise lies in a term of the time, "Tom o' Bedlam," referring to a feigned or real "mad" beggar, presumed to have been released recently from Bethlehem Royal (Mental) Hospital, commonly called Bedlam, outside the walls of London. A popular ballad of the time, "Tom o' Bedlam," specifically refers to mad singing, begging, and nakedness.
82 Reinforcing themes.
83 Heightening the awareness of opposites; the specific nature of one is played off against that of another.
84 This is a device whereby the playwright allows the audience to know more than the characters.
85 Imagery underlines the main themes of a play in a non-verbal manner.
86 A motif in literature is a recurring device that has a symbolic significance and underlines and expands the main themes.
87 Foreshadowing is a kind of dramatic irony where the full truth of a statement becomes apparent only with hindsight.
88 Iambic pentameter is poetry written in lines of ten syllables with five beats. This sounds like a heartbeat or a horse galloping; it is a basic human rhythm: da-DUM da-DUM da-DUM da-DUM da-DUM.
89 We distinguish between *metre* and *rhythm*. *Metre* is the underlying pattern of stressed and unstressed syllables—in Shakespeare mainly (iambic) blank verse. *Rhythm* is a feature of natural spoken language, which can subtly shift the metre. The interaction between metre and rhythm accentuates the meaning and creates tension in the spoken verse, so that it sounds like natural speech.
90 *The Iliad*, Book XVIII.

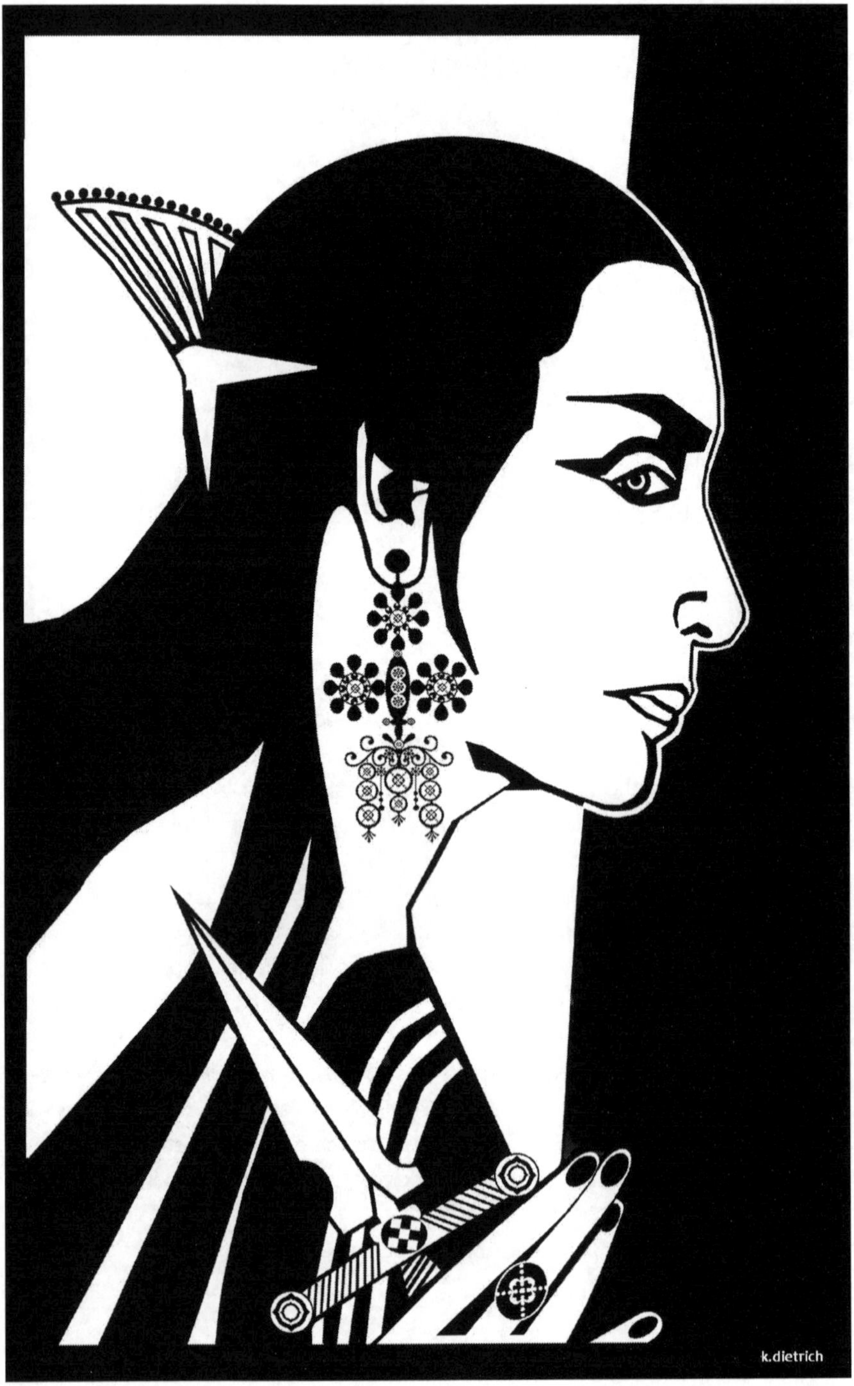
k.dietrich

CHAPTER V

MACBETH (1606)

"He who acquires such a State, if he means to keep it, must see ...that the blood of the ancient line of Princes be destroyed."
—Nicolò Machiavelli, *The Prince*

"The Scottish play," as *Macbeth* is sometimes called, is the last of the four great tragedies, written in 1606, three years after James I ascended the throne. James had previously been King James VI of Scotland and now strove to unite the kingdoms of England and Scotland. He even introduced a combined flag made up of both countries' national flags, the beginnings of the Union Jack.

James had more than a passing interest in witches and had published a book entitled *Demonology*. He had been present at the trials of women accused of witchcraft and knew of their being burned at the stake. In his book he also suggested ways of dealing with witches.

Furthermore, *Macbeth* was written in the immediate

aftermath of the Gunpowder Treason Plot in 1605 by Catholic rebels with the aim of blowing up the king and the House of Lords.

There was a real Macbeth. He lived in eleventh-century Scotland, and this is the setting for the play. The historic Macbeth has remarkably little in common with the tragic hero of Shakespeare's play. As we have noted, Shakespeare was not interested in historical fact but rather in using historical settings to explore Elizabethan and Jacobean society. Here, as elsewhere, he used Holinshed's *Chronicles* as a source.

1. THE PLOT

The play opens with a frightening witch scene, setting an atmosphere of evil. The witches' parting chant, "Fair is foul, and foul is fair" (1.1.12), articulates an important aspect of this play.

The plot proper begins with King Duncan receiving news of Macbeth's bravery and victory in battle over the rebel Macdonwald and, immediately afterwards, the King of Norway. Hearing of the treachery of the Thane of Cawdor, Duncan orders his execution and awards Macbeth this title in his stead.

Macbeth, returning from battle with his friend Banquo, comes across the witches, who have been expecting him. They hail Macbeth's rise to the position of Thane of Cawdor and indeed to king. Banquo asks about his own future, only to hear that his children, not he, will be kings.[91] After Macbeth receives news of his promotion he engages with the witches' prophecies and directly and secretly contemplates the murder of Duncan.

He writes his wife a letter telling her of the prophecy. The king and his entourage decide to stay the night at Macbeth's castle; Macbeth rides ahead.

Lady Macbeth decides after reading the letter that everything must be done to make her husband king. She realises that this will require ruthlessness, and that Macbeth's "human kindness" (1.5.16) may be an obstacle. When Macbeth arrives she insists that Duncan's assassination[92] must take place that night.

After all are gone to bed, Macbeth meets Banquo, who cannot sleep because of "cursèd thoughts" (2.1.8).

Despite great qualms, Macbeth goes ahead with the murder.

A knocking on the door in the early morning causes the Macbeths to retreat to their bedchamber and brings out the porter to answer the door. This short scene brings comic relief to the rising drama. Outside are Macduff and Lennox to meet Duncan. Macduff discovers the dead king. In the ensuing confusion Macbeth kills, as suspects, the two servants who had been sleeping in Duncan's chamber.

Duncan's sons, Malcolm and Donalbain, who had also stayed in the castle, quickly sense treachery: "There's daggers in men's smiles. The near in blood, | The nearer bloody" (2.3.136–137). They flee to England and Ireland, respectively.

Macbeth acts with great speed and resolve. He is proclaimed king at Scone,[93] and a banquet is planned to celebrate.

Meanwhile Banquo suspects foul play. Although Macbeth asks Banquo to be at the banquet, he has already met murderers and has commissioned the killing of his friend and his son, Fleance, in an effort to put a stop to Banquo's line of succession.

As Banquo dies he realises fully Macbeth's "treachery" (3.3.18). Fleance escapes, and Banquo indeed appears at the banquet—as a blood-covered ghost in Macbeth's seat. Only Macbeth sees the ghost, and an emotionally charged scene ensues.

Macbeth's dreadful distress causes great upset for the invited nobles and requires much effort on the part of Lady Macbeth to explain it away. The nobles are sent home, and the Macbeths talk briefly before retiring.

Macbeth realises that he has reached a point of no return. He says he needs to act without compunction.

This is the last time Lady Macbeth appears before she loses her mind and is tormented in her sleepwalking.

A scene with Lennox and another lord makes it clear that they suspect Macbeth of murdering Duncan and Banquo. They know that Malcolm is at the English court of Edward I, preparing an army to free Scotland. They also confirm that Macduff is on the run.

Macbeth seeks out the witches to discover more of his future. They reveal to him three apparitions. The first is in the shape of an "armed head," warning him of Macduff. The second apparition, in the shape of a "bloody child," announces: "Be bloody, bold and resolute . . . none of woman born | Shall harm Macbeth" (4.1.79–81). Finally, "a child crowned, with a tree in his hand" appears and prophesies that "Macbeth shall never vanquished be until | Great Birnam Wood to high Dunsinane Hill | Shall come against him" (4.1.92–94). All this suggests to Macbeth that he is invincible and that he must pursue Macduff.

At Macbeth's persistent questioning regarding the descendants of Banquo, a further vision is evoked of "eight kings, the last with a glass in his hand, followed by Banquo" (stage direction, following line 4.1.111).

When Macbeth hears that Macduff has fled to England he

resolves to extinguish his entire line:

> The castle of Macduff I will surprise,
> Seize upon Fife, give to th' edge o' th' sword
> His wife, his babes, and all unfortunate souls
> That trace him in his line.
>
> (4.1.151–154)

Between this resolve and its execution there is a humorous scene in which we meet Lady Macduff and her son. This interlude is turned into the sheer horror of a child being killed on stage.

Meanwhile Macduff has met Malcolm at the English court. Malcolm tests Macduff's honesty and allegiance by pretending to be viler than Macbeth. Edward I, the anointed English king, performs miracle healings of an illness called "the evil."

Ross arrives from Scotland and brings Macduff the news of the slaughter of his family. They prepare to march the ready army to Scotland.

In Scotland a "waiting-gentlewoman" (servant) consults a doctor about Lady Macbeth's sleepwalking, and we witness this terror-fraught somnambulism on stage. The doctor and the woman understand from Lady Macbeth's behaviour and utterances that the cause is a deep emotional disturbance related to the killing of Duncan and Lady Macduff.

The doctor speaks to Macbeth as he prepares for battle. Macbeth asks the doctor to cure his wife of "the memory of a rooted sorrow" (5.3.43), but when the doctor replies that he cannot help, Macbeth's thoughts turn to the approaching conflict.

As the English army draws near, Macbeth hears the news of

his wife's death. But he has become too callous to care. The army moves towards his castle, holding branches from Birnam Wood as camouflage, as the second apparition had enigmatically foretold. Macbeth becomes unnerved by the apparent truth of the apparitions.

He is finally undone by the fact that Macduff, who was born by Caesarean section, challenges him. This is the man, "none of woman born," fated to defeat Macbeth. They battle off stage, and Macduff appears with Macbeth's head. At the end of the play, Duncan's son Malcolm, who has led the victorious army, is proclaimed King of Scotland.

2. WHO ARE THE CHARACTERS?

MACBETH

Macbeth dominates the play. He is the character we get to know best, in his thinking, his misgivings, his development. This is because of the many soliloquies and asides, which trace his innermost feelings from the start.

The first reports of him are of his valour in battle; he is proclaimed noble and worthy. His first words, "So fair and foul a day" (1.3.38), echo the witches: "Fair is foul and foul is fair" (1.1.12). Macbeth immediately engages with the witches and their prophecies after he is given the news of his promotion to be Thane of Cawdor, saying to himself, "The greatest is behind" (1.3.119), that is, coming after this. Seconds later this thought has turned to the possibility of killing the king to bring about his advancement:

> ... why do I yield to that suggestion

> Whose horrid image doth unfix my hair
> And make my seated heart knock at my ribs
>
> (1.3.136–138)

These secret thoughts show the spectators a part of the hero that is not at all apparent to the other characters in the play.

Yet, unlike the Machiavellian characters in the earlier tragedies, Macbeth harbours a sense of remorse. He is not outright evil: he is a more complex person and not entirely void of human compassion:

> My thought, whose murder yet is but fantastical,
> Shakes so my single state of man
> That function is smothered in surmise,
> And nothing is but what is not.
>
> (1.3.141–144)

The only person Macbeth trusts and is open with is his wife, his "dearest partner in greatness" (1.5.10–11). Macbeth's love for his wife is an important part of his human kindness. The Machiavellian characters in the other tragedies loved nobody apart from themselves. The capacity for love of another person is an indicator of humanity.

Macbeth writes to his wife about the witches' prophecy and shares his secret ambition with her: "what greatness is promised thee" (1.5.12–13). Lady Macbeth's first soliloquy, after reading the letter, reveals her insight into Macbeth's character. She realises both his ambition and his compassionate side.

Macbeth's fearful struggles within himself find expression in his open and truthful conversations with his wife and also in his soliloquies, which frequently take the shape of hallucinations, until the banquet scene.

Two of these soliloquies occur before Macbeth commits the murder of Duncan and nearly prevent him from carrying it out. However, Lady Macbeth urges him on. When he tells her about killing Duncan he is particularly upset that he couldn't say "Amen" (2.2.24–30) when the servants blessed themselves.

Again, Lady Macbeth counsels prophetically: "These deeds must not be thought | After these ways. So, it will make us mad" (2.2.31–32). Macbeth's torment after the killing takes the shape of a hallucination. He has heard a voice cry, "Sleep no more! Macbeth does murder sleep" (2.2.33–34), and believes he will never be able to wash the blood from his hands.

After the discovery of the murder Macbeth is proclaimed king at Scone, and he prepares with his wife for the banquet. He has learnt from her the effectiveness of appearing different from how he feels inside and agrees with her that they will "make our faces vizards to our hearts, | Disguising what they are" (3.2.35–36).

Although he hints at Banquo and Fleance being the new threat to his kingship, he does not reveal to Lady Macbeth that he has already hired assassins to eliminate them. Macbeth's readiness to kill children is significant. He orders the killing not only of Fleance but also, not long after this, of all Macduff's children. There is something heinous about the slaughter of children.

The banquet scene is the last time we see Macbeth struggling with tormenting hallucinations, this time as he imagines that the ghost of Banquo sits in his chair at the table.

The guests are sent away to avoid Macbeth giving himself away, and he concludes the scene by saying:

> ... I am in blood
> Stepped in so far that, should I wade no more,
> Returning were as tedious as go o'er
>
> (3.4.136–138)

This marks a new stage in Macbeth's descent.

Another visit to the witches seems to Macbeth to establish that he has nothing and nobody to fear except for Macduff. We witness no more pangs of conscience; we see and hear about Scotland's decline into bloody warfare and a rule of terror.

As Macbeth prepares to take on and fight the English army led by Malcolm, he reveals an honest understanding of where his tyranny has brought him:

> And that which should accompany old age,
> As honour, love, obedience, troops of friends,
> I must not look to have, but, in their stead,
> Curses
>
> (5.3.26–29)

There is even a suggestion at this point that life has lost all meaning for Macbeth, and he feels in his heart that he would gladly end it: "breath | Which the poor heart would fain deny and dare not" (5.3.29–30).

Perhaps the greatest measure of Macbeth's loss of humanity is the loss of his love for his wife. We do not see him again with her after the banquet, when he declares he will continue on his bloody path.

Macbeth is insensitive to his wife's death and comments about life in a vein that is opposite to the Renaissance vision: "Life's | . . . a tale | Told by an idiot, full of sound and fury, |

Signifying nothing" (5.5.24–28). This is Macbeth's tragedy. Life has lost all meaning for him. He has lost the love of his life, joy and happiness, friends; only this realisation is evidence of some shred of remaining humanity, of a humane core. The cause of this destruction is Macbeth's Machiavellian ambition.

LADY MACBETH

Lady Macbeth is introduced reading Macbeth's letter and through her first soliloquy, responding to the letter. This reveals her insight into Macbeth's character:

> . . . Yet I do fear thy nature;
> It is too full o' th' milk of human kindness
> . . .
> Art not without ambition
>
> (1.5.16–18)

In her second soliloquy she reveals that she too has a sense of wrongdoing in her murderous scheming:

> . . . Come, you spirits
> That tend to mortal thoughts, unsex me here,
> . . .
> Stop up the access and passage to remorse,
> That no compunctious visitings of nature
> Shake my fell purpose
>
> (1.5.41–47)

A measure of Lady Macbeth's, and indeed Macbeth's, capacity for inhumanity is their readiness to kill children. Lady

Macbeth declares:

> ... I have given suck, and know
> How tender 'tis to love the babe that milks me.
> I would, while it was smiling in my face,
> Have plucked my nipple from his boneless gums
> And dashed the brains out, had I so sworn as you
> Have done to this.
>
> (1.7.54–59)

Here we have again, before her statement of her capacity for inhumanity, the potential she has for giving and receiving human kindness. Lady Macbeth's development during the play doubles that of Macbeth. She also harbours some humanity, which she is aware of and determines to eliminate, so that it will not hinder her purpose.

In the first half of the play she is the stronger of the two in Machiavellian purpose. It takes all her powers of persuasion to keep Macbeth to his purpose of killing Duncan. However, she commits none of the killings and is not fully in the picture about any murders after that of Duncan. Tellingly, she states that she might have stabbed Duncan to death had "he not resembled | My father as he slept" (2.2.12–13).

However, she forces Macbeth to commit murder, especially by taunting him that he is not a real man if he has second thoughts about killing his kinsman, guest, and king. It is Lady Macbeth who plans the details of the killing of Duncan, placing the bloody daggers beside Duncan's servants and smearing them with blood.

The last moment of closeness between Macbeth and his wife comes just before and during the banquet. They are both dressed in their royal robes after the coronation. Macbeth protects his wife from the knowledge that he has commissioned the murder of Banquo and Fleance.

During the banquet, when Macbeth suffers his terrible hallucinations, Lady Macbeth makes an enormous effort to calm him and the alarmed guests. She is clearly stretched beyond her emotional limits, and she disappears from the play until we see her again towards the end, having lost her peace of mind.

After the banquet scene Lady Macbeth is apparently unable to continue on the bloody road taken by her husband. We next hear of her when the woman who attends her speaks to a doctor about her tormented sleepwalking, and we witness such an episode. Lady Macbeth compulsively rubs her hands, reliving Macbeth's fears of not being able to wash the blood off: "What, will these hands ne'er be clean" (5.1.36–37). Her words consist of repetitions of what she said to Macbeth to humiliate him, Macbeth's fears, and her own honest horror at the deeds she has been complicit in: "who would have thought the old man to have had so much blood in him" (5.1.33–34).

She has clearly heard about the slaughter of Macduff's family: "The thane of Fife had a wife. Where is she now" (5.1.36). Everything is mixed up in the night terrors. At the end of the play it is reported that Lady Macbeth has committed suicide, an option also considered by her husband as a way out of his torment. While in Macbeth's case the agony arises from a life that means nothing to him any more, Lady Macbeth's suffering comes from a realisation of her complicity in a reign of terror and murder. Although she personally did not take the life of anybody, there is a profound understanding that she too has blood on her hands.

DUNCAN

Duncan represents the values of the old Elizabethan and Jacobean nobility, and shares their naïveté. He believes in the loyalty of his subjects and is not prepared for treachery. Although he declares that one can tell a villain by looking at him—"There is no art | To find the mind's construction in the face" (1.4.12–13)—he nevertheless believes in people's appearance and is gullible; he is not equipped to deal with the Machiavellian deceiver.

Like Lear, Duncan is cherished by his loyal subjects. His murder is viewed as a crime and unleashes tyranny, wars, and destitution.

Malcolm and his brother Donalbain understand that their father has been murdered. They realise that this is not the work of drunken servants but is a planned attack on the royal line, with the purpose of usurpation. They know they must flee right away in order to save their lives: "This murderous shaft that's shot | Hath not yet lighted, and our safest way | Is to avoid the aim" (2.3.137–139). Their astuteness is a necessary quality in dealing with the usurper and is essential to good kingship.

While Donalbain leaves the play at this point, Malcolm develops into the future leader. He flees to King Edward's court in England and there is helped by Edward and other nobles to recruit a loyal army.

EDWARD

Edward is a Christ-like king. He is pious and cures people of illness, including the one called "the king's evil"—an actual disease[94] —as well as having the metaphorical ability to cure evil per se. Malcolm's alignment with Edward, and the support he gains from the people of Northumberland and their Lord Siward, demonstrate that he is the rightful heir to the throne of Scotland. Furthermore, this potential for a good relationship between England and Scotland was in the interests of, and was personified by, James I.

MALCOLM

Malcolm is developed as a model Christian prince in Erasmus's terms.[95] This is shown in the sovereignty with which he plans and carries out the liberation of Scotland from its tyrant. All the qualities needed in a good king and leader of a nation are also spelt out in an amusing scene between Malcolm and Macduff. Malcolm understands that he must be wary of treachery, and so he tests Macduff's honesty and loyalty. In this scene he pretends to be worse than Macbeth:

> ... The king-becoming graces,
> As justice, verity, temperance, stableness,
> Bounty, perseverance, mercy, lowliness,
> Devotion, patience, courage, fortitude,
> I have no relish of them
> ... had I power, I should
> Pour the sweet milk of concord into hell,
> Uproar the universal peace, confound
> All unity on earth.
>
> (4.3. 93–102)

Malcolm lists all the "king-becoming graces" only to deny he has them. In fact, he claims, he would destroy world peace.

When Ross brings Macduff the shocking news of his family's complete eradication by Macbeth's henchmen, Malcolm responds very personally and kindly to Macduff's grief: "Give sorrow words. The grief that does not speak | Whispers the o'erfraught heart and bids it break" (4.3.211–212).

Malcolm's intelligence is further evidenced when he orders his army to camouflage itself with branches from Birnam Wood.

When Macduff comes on stage with Macbeth's head, Malcolm changes the ancient Scottish title of Thane to the English Earl. He promises to reverse the tyranny and restore Scotland to its former self:

> ... calling home our exiled friends abroad
> That fled the snares of watchful tyranny,
> Producing forth the cruel ministers
> Of this dead butcher and his fiendlike queen
> (5.8.66–69)

There is no doubt at the end of the play that the alliance with England was good for Scotland and essential to the defeat of the evil that had invaded it.

BANQUO

Banquo is the next-greatest threat after Duncan's sons in Macbeth's eyes, as his children are prophesied future kings. Yet he does not take precautions—despite growing doubts: "Thou hast it now: king, Cawdor, Glamis, all, | As the weird women promised, and I fear | Thou played'st most foully for't" (3.1.1–3). However, he realises the full extent of Macbeth's "treachery" (3.3.18) only when he is assassinated, telling his son: "Fly, good

Fleance, fly, fly, fly! | Thou may'st revenge" (3.3.18–19).

LENNOX

After the death of Banquo, and observing Macbeth at the banquet, Lennox is present at important times. He observes Macbeth after the murder of Duncan is discovered, and he is the one who is close at hand during the banquet scene, when Banquo's ghost takes Macbeth's seat.

As events unfold further, Lennox speaks sarcastically to another lord:

> And the right-valiant Banquo walked too late,
> Whom, you may say, if 't please you, Fleance killed,
> For Fleance fled. Men must not walk too late.
> Who cannot want the thought how monstrous
> It was for Malcolm and for Donalbain
> To kill their gracious father? Damnèd fact!
> How it did grieve Macbeth! Did he not straight
> In pious rage the two delinquents tear
> That were the slaves of drink and thralls of sleep?
> Was not that nobly done? Ay, and wisely too
>
> (3.6.5–14)

This is deeply ironic and amuses the audience. While Lennox remains in Scotland for a while, he later joins Malcolm's army.

ROSS

Ross brings Macbeth the news of his accession as Thane of Cawdor. He too is at the banquet and, like Lennox, is unsuspecting.

This has changed by the time he goes to warn Lady Macduff that her husband has fled, indicating that Scotland has gone out of control under Macbeth:

> I dare not speak much further;
> But cruel are the times when we are traitors
> And do not know ourselves; when we hold rumour
> From what we fear, yet know not what we fear
> (4.2.17–20)

A reign of terror has been unleashed in Scotland, and Ross comments on this most vividly throughout the remainder of the play. He is the noble who will bring Macduff the news that all his family have been killed.

MACDUFF

Macduff undergoes a development similar to that of the other Scottish nobles, Banquo, Lennox, and Ross. At first he, like the others, does not suspect Macbeth of foul play. All lack the astuteness of Duncan's sons.

Macduff incurs Macbeth's displeasure by not appearing at Scone or for his celebratory banquet. Macbeth's suspicions seem to be confirmed by the witches, who warn him, "Beware Macduff" (4.1.71).

Shakespeare imprints the murder of Macduff's family on us by inserting a short scene beforehand in which Lady Macduff and her son have an entertaining exchange, debating "What is a traitor?" (4.2.46). This scene endears the courageous little boy to the audience, who feel his murder on stage all the more now that they have got to know and love him.

Directly after this we see the unsuspecting Macduff speak to Malcolm at the English court, where Malcolm tests his loyalty in an amusing pretence of vileness. Here Macduff makes it clear that his loyalty to his country is greater even than to his king. He makes allowances for Malcolm's pretended "voluptuousness" and "avarice" (4.3.62, 80). However, Malcolm's final assertion, that he would destroy world peace, is so unacceptable to Macduff that he loses all hope and he calls out:

> O Scotland, Scotland!
> . . .
> These evils thou repeat'st upon thyself
> Have banished me from Scotland.—O my breast,
> Thy hope ends here!
>
> (4.3.102–116)

This comes just before he hears of the slaughter of his family. Macduff's grief-stricken words "At one fell swoop?" (4.3.224) have since entered everyday English idiom. This murder of Macduff's wife and children gives him a degree of parity with Malcolm. They each enact part of the witches' prophecies in a scientifically reasonable way: Malcolm devises a tactical military manoeuvre (the camouflaging branches) while we learn that Macduff was born by Caesarean section ("man not born of woman"). Jointly they destroy Macbeth, with Macduff engaging in the final physical combat and taking his head.

THE PORTER

The porter should not go unremarked. He is the clown figure in the play, the one who pronounces truth.

The porter scene follows the killing of Duncan, preceded by all Macbeth's struggles with himself and his wife. The great irony is that the porter is playing the role of the "porter of hell-gate" (2.3.1)—a truth not even apparent to himself. The audience enjoy their inside knowledge, which adds to the drama, giving the porter's words additional significance.

Apocalyptic knocking accompanies his fantasies about the kind of people he would admit to Hell—all of them deceivers of some kind, known to the spectators from their own society. Before he opens the door he says: "I had thought to have let in some of all professions that go the primrose way to the everlasting bonfire" (2.3.16–18).

The porter's insight has parallels with Macduff's son's quizzing of his mother regarding the nature of a traitor. Lady Macduff's definition, "one that swears and lies" (4.2.47), sounds not unlike the porter's line-up for Hell. In the same vein Lady Macduff tells her son that every traitor "must be hanged" (4.2.49) by "the honest men" (4.2.53), whereupon her son concludes: "Then the liars and swearers are fools, for there are liars and swearers enough to beat the honest men and hang up them" (4.2.54–55).

Macduff's son can be seen therefore as a doubling of the porter, with a fool's licence to tell the truth where others dare not. They both inhabit comic scenes that punctuate the drama. Also, importantly, Shakespeare undermines, as he often does, class boundaries. The porter and the child of the nobility are presented as having the same viewpoint and sharing a common humanity.

When the porter finally opens the door, Lennox and Macduff enter. The crime is as yet undiscovered, and so the inebriated porter has a bit more ribald fun with the two nobles, no doubt to the delight of the audience.

THE WITCHES

Witches were considered a reality by many people in Shakespeare's day. Their appearance throughout the play must have added a thrilling sense of horror to an already demonic atmosphere. They are an amazing piece of dramatic invention.

The witches in *Macbeth* possess supernatural powers. They know they will meet Macbeth, and they play tricks on him, exploiting his ambition. However, it is interesting to see how characters who in some respect double Macbeth—Banquo and Lady Macbeth, in very different ways—react to the "weird sisters" (1.3.32).

Banquo, on first meeting them along with Macbeth, repeatedly asks who they are and what they are, adopting scientific disbelief:

> I' th' name of truth,
> Are ye fantastical, or that indeed
> Which outwardly ye show?
>
> (1.3.53–55)

He also tests them in what they have to say about his future, insisting that he is not afraid of them: "me, who neither beg nor fear | Your favours nor your hate" (1.3.61–62). On the whole, Banquo is less inclined to give credence to the witches' prophecies: "Were such things here as we do speak about? | Or have we eaten on the insane root | That takes the reason prisoner" (1.3.84–86).

Macbeth, on the other hand, engages immediately and fully

with their prophecies. As we have seen, his thoughts turn to murder almost as soon as he receives news of his promotion to Thane of Cawdor, believing this to be in part fulfilment of the prophecy.

When Banquo begins to suspect Macbeth of foul play, he places the responsibility squarely with Macbeth, and not with the witches.

Lady Macbeth is also not especially interested in the witches. Their prophecies suit her, and therefore she doesn't challenge their validity. She never asks to see the witches, nor does she express any fear of them. In fact Lady Macbeth herself is a doubling of the witches—a more real and dangerous one.

Had Banquo not seen the witches at first, together with Macbeth, they might simply have been a trick of Macbeth's highly imaginative mind. Banquo disregards the witches. Nobody else sees them. When Macbeth seeks them out a second time, after the banquet, Lennox crosses his path immediately afterwards. Lennox assures him he saw nothing.

So, only Macbeth engages with the witches. He is fascinated and wants to believe them, because they appeal to a part of his character: his ambition. Nothing in his rise and fall would have been different without the witches, except that it might have taken him a little longer to plot the murder of Duncan. The truly evil happenings, on stage and off stage, are directly connected to the Macbeths.

3. WHAT IS THE PLAY ABOUT?

THE STRUGGLE AGAINST MACHIAVELLIANISM

The struggle between human kindness and the ruthless pursuit of power lies at the heart of this play and defines the specific nature of the play's tragic hero. Here, for the first time in Shakespeare's tragedies, we have the struggle to the death taking place within one person.

No longer is the Machiavellian factor personified by one or more characters seeking the fall of the Renaissance humanist (Hamlet or Othello) or out to destroy the feudal nobility (Lear). Macbeth is a more complex character than those who are cast in the Vice tradition of the morality plays, because he destroys himself.

This is doubled by Lady Macbeth, who also makes an effort to suppress any humane feelings within herself in the Machiavellian pursuit of power. The love the Macbeths have for one another transcends the pure Vice character. It is the ability to have regard for another person outside the self that makes the Macbeths human and that is their potential. However, their ambition compels them to slaughter all in their way, even children—the future of humanity. It destroys the Macbeths, their innate capacity for love and kindness, and their deeply hidden understanding that they are humanity's anathema.

GOOD KINGSHIP

What is needed in a good king is shown above all in Malcolm and Edward, who have the ability to deal with the usurper and terrorist leader. A good king or leader must put the well-being of their nation above all else. They have to be wise, compassionate, and fearless in the face of evil.

4. THE DRAMA OF IT ALL

Just how Shakespeare makes Macbeth an exciting play can be

studied in his use of a variety of dramatic devices. Among these are:

DOUBLING[97]

• At first Macbeth and Banquo are both valiant captains in Duncan's army, and are friends. Macbeth talks to Banquo about the witches but distances himself inwardly from him after he engages with the witches' prophecy. Macbeth and Banquo show different ways of responding to the witches.
• Macbeth and Lady Macbeth undergo similar yet converse developments. Macbeth is tormented in the first half of the play by his conscience; this happens to Lady Macbeth only after the enormity of what she has supported sinks in, and causes her agony. Macbeth starts out that way but later becomes as callous as Lady Macbeth is at the beginning.
• Macduff's son and the porter double each other as "fools," who have a similar insight into the deceptions of society. They say what they think.
• Lady Macbeth doubles the witches in the fear she instils. However, she is far more real than they are, and more capable of participating in evil.

CONTRAST[98]

• The Machiavellian Macbeths v. the old nobility (for example Duncan) v. the humanist forces of Malcolm, Edward, Macduff, etc.
• The sequences of very different scenes: for example the witches scene followed by Duncan, or Duncan arriving after Macbeth and Lady Macbeth plan to murder him that night in their castle.

- Sequences where comic scenes follow high tension, as a form of relief: the porter scene following the murder of Duncan, the scene between Lady Macduff and her son preceding their murder.

DRAMATIC IRONY[99]

- This is often found in soliloquies or asides, where a character reveals inner thoughts to the audience, often making them aware of things that the characters in the play are ignorant of—for example Macbeth's early intention of murdering not only Duncan but also Malcolm.
- It can also be situational irony, with the appearance of characters in telling situations—for example Macbeth's appearance on stage after Duncan says of the traitor Cawdor, "He was a gentleman on whom I built | An absolute trust." Enter Macbeth. (1.4.13–14).
- It can also manifest itself as verbal irony, where the playwright knows the future of a character or a situation that the characters themselves, and the audience, are unaware of—for example Macbeth's reaction to the death of Duncan:

> Had I but died an hour before this chance,
> I had lived a blessèd time, for from this instant
> There's nothing serious in mortality.
> All is but toys. Renown and grace is dead.
>
> (2.3.86–89)

This insincere speech anticipates ironically Macbeth's own observation on the meaninglessness of life at the end of his bloody career.

IMAGERY[100]

- Blood is perhaps the starkest of images in this play. It first appears on the imaginary dagger in Macbeth's hallucination before Duncan's murder, and again as something he cannot ever wash off his hands. Then there is Banquo's blood-covered ghost at the banquet, and at the end of this scene Macbeth's comment that having gone so far in the river of blood he might as well go on. Other people also use blood to describe the state of Scotland under Macbeth's rule; Macduff cries out: "Bleed, bleed, poor country" (4.3.32).
- Darkness and light: Many scenes take place in the dark or at night. Both Macbeth and Lady Macbeth call on the night to cover their deeds: "Stars, hide your fires; | Let not light see my black and deep desires." (1.4.52–53) and "Come, thick night, | And pall thee in the dunnest smoke of hell, | That my keen knife see not the wound it makes" (1.5.51–53). Much later, Lady Macbeth cannot sleep without a light by her bed.
- Sickness and healing: Here especially there is King Edward's ability to heal the "king's evil" and the doctor's inability to heal Lady Macbeth of mental torment caused by her evil actions and her support of Macbeth's murders.
- Animal imagery is used throughout the play to comment on horror. In this example it is used to spell out unnaturalness on the night of Duncan's murder: "A falcon tow'ring in her pride of place, | Was by a mousing owl hawked at and killed" (2.4.12–13) and "Duncan's horses . . . | Make war with mankind. 'Tis said they eat each other." (2.4.14–18).

MOTIF[101]

- Hallucinations and sleepwalking: These are Macbeth's and Lady Macbeth's manifestations of conscience—their realisation that they are violating humanity by their reign of terror. Both of

them realise that murder is wrong and irredeemable.
- Sleeplessness: Sleep and lack of sleep are mentioned several times in the play. Sound sleep is regarded as a sign of a clear conscience and of healing:

> ...—the innocent sleep,
> Sleep that knits up the raveled sleave of care,
> The death of each day's life, sore labour's bath,
> Balm of hurt minds, great nature's second course,
> Chief nourisher in life's feast.
> (2.2.34–38)

Neither Banquo nor Macbeth can sleep properly on the night before Duncan's murder. The most striking manifestation of an inability to sleep resulting from tormented conscience is Lady Macbeth's sleepwalking.

FORESHADOWING[102]

- Lady Macbeth's concern about Macbeth being too full of "the milk of human kindness" is borne out in his many anxieties and hallucinations, verging on madness.
- Lady Macbeth's wish for spirits to "Stop up the access and passage to remorse, | That no compunctious visitings of nature | Shake my fell purpose" (1.5.45–47) foreshadows the fact that this is ultimately unsuccessful. She too contains a core of human kindness.
- Banquo's sleeplessness foreshadows death and Lady Macbeth's night terrors.

5. CLOSE FOCUS: THE BANQUET SCENE

ACT 3, SCENE 4

The banquet scene comes right in the middle of the play. It is the last time we see Macbeth struggling with his humane instincts in contrast to his Machiavellian ambition. It is also the last time that we see Macbeth and Lady Macbeth together in the happy company of others. All these factors are significant in the developing plot, and Shakespeare employs a variety of devices to heighten dramatic tension at this point.

The scene directly follows the murder of Banquo. This in itself is a dramatic juxtaposing of a scene in darkness and of murder with a brightly lit banqueting-hall, a celebratory dinner of many lords in honour of Macbeth's coronation.

It is also profoundly ironic, as it states the opposite of what the audience know is true: Macbeth is a usurper and killer. Further irony occurs throughout the scene. An instance of verbal irony is Macbeth's comment early on that he will "play the humble host" (4). Play he does indeed, but humble he is not.

Only a few moments into this scene Banquo's murderer appears at the door of the banqueting-hall, and Macbeth has to play two roles: that of host and that of himself conversing secretly with the assassin, who tells him that, while Banquo is dead, Fleance has escaped. This shocks Macbeth. As the assassin exits, Lady Macbeth comes over to Macbeth and encourages him to take part in the feast. She is unaware of the death of Banquo.

Macbeth joins the festivities and is invited by Lennox to sit down, when Banquo's ghost appears in his seat. Shakespeare's directions are clear: that the ghost should sit in Macbeth's place. Before Macbeth turns to his seat he declares:

> Here had we now our country's honour roofed,
> Were the graced person of our Banquo present
>
> (40–41)

This is highly dramatic, as Banquo has apparently followed this invitation and appeared in his present state—dead. The tension spirals when the audience realise that only Macbeth sees the ghost.

Ross and Lady Macbeth realise that something is happening to Macbeth, Lady Macbeth making light of it, explaining that Macbeth often has fits. Regardless of the enormity of the situation, Macbeth continues to speak to Banquo's ghost.

In contrast to Macbeth's previous hallucinations, where the spectators did not share his visions, they now see the ghost and therefore the reality of Macbeth's imaginings. They are put in his shoes and perhaps feel with him the horror of what he has done. Here Macbeth is literally confronted with the reality of the murder: Banquo sits there and does not speak. This is highly dramatic.

Macbeth compromises himself in speaking to the ghost. When the ghost vanishes, Macbeth recovers himself somewhat, returns to his guests, and drinks a toast, ironically "love and health to all" (87), which is the opposite of what Scotland will experience at the hands of Macbeth.

Again, Banquo's ghost appears just before Macbeth states once more that he wishes Banquo were present:

> I drink to the general joy o' th' whole table,
> And to our dear friend Banquo, whom we miss;
> Would he were here! To all and him . . .
>
> (89–91)

As Macbeth becomes aware of the ghost he is again caught off guard, and Lady Macbeth tries to reassure the lords. The ghost vanishes when Macbeth shouts, "Hence" (106). As Macbeth can no longer be controlled, or relied upon not to say the wrong things, Lady Macbeth hurries out their guests.

Macbeth reiterates his superstitious bent, which Lady Macbeth never engages with: "Blood will have blood. | Stones have been known to move, and trees to speak" (122–23).

He also tells her he has placed spies everywhere—"There's not a one of them but in his house | I keep a servant fee'd" (131–32)—and that he is suspicious of Macduff. He also confides in her that he will be seeking out the witches in the early morning. Most importantly, at the end of this fraught scene Macbeth has decided that he will continue on his bloody path. He reassures his wife that he will overcome his sensitivities as they become more practised in crime.

All these intimations will be more fully developed as the drama continues, except that Lady Macbeth will not become more hardened to murder.

6. NOTE THE LANGUAGE

As in all his plays, in Macbeth Shakespeare mainly uses blank verse in iambic pentameter[103], and prose. Blank verse is usually reserved for the speech of the nobility. Here Ross is talking to an "old man" about the way night has encompassed day:[104]

> Thou seest, the heavens, as troubled with man's act,
> Threatens his bloody stage: by the clock, 'tis day,
> And yet dark night strangles the travelling lamp.
> Is't night's predominance or the day's shame

> That darkness does the face of Earth entomb
> When living light should kiss it?
>
> (2.4.5–10)

Prose is typically used for characters of a lower class or indeed for the mad. The porter speaks entirely in prose.

> Here's a knocking indeed! If a man were a porter of hell-gate, he should have old turning the key.
>
> (2.3.1–2)

Lady Macbeth's sleepwalking torment is further underlined in her speaking in prose:

> Here's the smell of blood still. All the perfumes of Arabia will not sweeten this little hand. Oh, Oh, Oh!
>
> (5.1.42–43)

THE BEAUTY OF THE LANGUAGE

Here Ross comments hauntingly on the state of Scotland under Macbeth's reign of terror:

> ... Alas, poor country!
> Almost afraid to know itself. It cannot
> Be call'd our mother, but our grave, where nothing,
> But who knows nothing, is once seen to smile;
> Where sighs and groans and shrieks that rend the air
> Are made, not marked; where violent sorrow seems
> A modern ecstasy. The dead man's knell

> Is there scarce asked for who, and good men's lives
> Expire before the flowers in their caps,
> Dying or ere they sicken.
>
> (4.3.166–175)

Often lines or passages in Shakespeare that resonate especially will echo through into different ages. John Keats, writing a little more than two hundred years after Shakespeare, and caring for his dying tubercular brother, Tom, echoed Ross's grief-stricken cry in his "Ode to a Nightingale":

> Fade far away, dissolve, and quite forget
> What thou among the leaves hast never known,
> The weariness, the fever, and the fret
> Here, where men sit and hear each other groan;
> Where palsy shakes a few, sad, last gray hairs,
> Where youth grows pale, and spectre-thin, and dies;
> Where but to think is to be full of sorrow
> And leaden-eyed despairs,
> Where Beauty cannot keep her lustrous eyes,
> Or new Love pine at them beyond to-morrow.

What links Keats with Shakespeare is the vision of a tomb-like society that is incommensurate with the need of humanity, where people are crushed.

7. THE ENDING

In this tragedy the tragic hero has destroyed himself, even before his physical end at the hands of Macduff.

Instead of achieving happiness through usurpation of the highest rank, Macbeth realises he has lost everything that makes life worth living: "honour, love, obedience, troops of friends" (5.3.27). He has succeeded in annihilating his own humanity, with life "signifying nothing" (5.5.28).

Lady Macbeth too extinguishes herself, even more literally than her husband, as she cannot bear the torment she endures every night, reliving the murders, for which she takes joint responsibility. It is interesting, and a further measure of her deeply hidden humanity, that she realises that she also has blood on her hands, even though she didn't actually kill anybody. Having been complicit in the murders makes her guilty, and this drives her into insanity.

Malcolm, who has led the victorious army and taken care of his loyal supporters, defended the welfare of Scotland, and displayed all the features of Erasmus's Christian prince, is proclaimed King of Scotland at the end of the play. In contrast to Hamlet and King Lear, the order of royal succession is restored. In Othello too the person to take over the position as leader in Cyprus, Cassio, is not necessarily the ideal Christian prince. But Malcolm is. He will restore order and happiness to Scotland. He has been shown to be an exemplary and wise leader.

8. CONCLUSIONS: WHAT IS THE TRAGEDY?

We have defined Shakespearean tragedy as the events leading to the undeserved downfall and death of a hero, caused ultimately by a Machiavellian power.

This is different in Macbeth. Here the humane core resides within the Machiavellian. We witness in this play the enormous destructive power of Machiavellian ambition. It is capable of eradicating humanity at the cost of annihilating itself. This vision is truly apocalyptic, and thoughts of our present times spring to mind.

Why are Macbeth and indeed Lady Macbeth tragic heroes? Because they possess the potential for human kindness, or humankind-ness. By destroying their humanity they become Machiavellian devils, and they cannot live with this. And so they die. That is their tragedy.

FOOTNOTES

91 James I was thought at the time to be a direct descendant of the real Banquo.
92 Shakespeare uses the word "assassination" only once in all his plays. It is the earliest known literary use of the word.
93 pronounced "Scoon."
94 Scrofula—a tubercular swelling of the lymph glands—was popularly called "the king's evil" because it was believed that only the touch of a king could cure it.
95 He is expected to "follow the right, do violence to no one, plunder no one, sell no public office, be corrupted by no bribes," as set out by Desiderius Erasmus in *The Education of a Christian Prince*, chapter I, "The qualities, education, and significance of a Christian prince."
96 Vice was one of the main stock characters in the medieval morality plays,[96] an agent of the Devil. The main character stood for the ordinary person and was often called Everyman. Another stock character was Virtue, representing the side of God. Vice and Virtue usually tried to win control over Everyman's soul. Vice frequently took the audience into his confidence, in soliloquies, by revealing his evil purpose.
97 reinforcing a theme by emphasis.
98 To heighten awareness of opposites, the specific nature of one is played off against that of another.
99 This is an irony inherent in speeches or a situation in a drama whereby the audience know more than most of the characters in the play.
100 Imagery underlines the main themes of a play in a non-verbal manner.
101 A motif in literature is a recurring device that has a symbolic significance and underlines and expands the main themes.
102 Foreshadowing is a kind of dramatic irony where the full truth of a statement becomes apparent only with hindsight.
103 Iambic pentameter is poetry written in lines of ten syllables with five beats. This sounds like a heartbeat or a horse galloping; it is a basic human rhythm: da-DUM da-DUM da-DUM da-DUM da-DUM.
104 We distinguish between metre and rhythm. Metre is the underlying pattern of stressed and unstressed syllables—in Shakespeare mainly (iambic) blank verse. Rhythm is a feature of natural spoken language, which can subtly shift the metre. The interaction between metre and rhythm accentuates the meaning and creates tension in the spoken verse, so that it sounds like natural speech.

CONCLUSIONS

Shakespeare lived at the beginning of the modern era, at the time of transition from feudalism to early capitalism. It was a time of unimaginable social upheaval, with old classes being overtaken by new ones. This unparalleled transformation, undermining so many old certainties, ushered in unstable and brutal times.

In an expression of their new historical place, the bourgeoisie developed both a humanist and a Machiavellian rationale. These are two sides of the same society, its potential for both a utopian and a totalitarian direction.

Shakespeare understood the nature of his society in a visionary way, a long time before anybody else. In the tragedies we have considered here, both potentials are put on stage, as well as characters caught in between. Interestingly, while we see a number of "pure" Machiavellians, few characters are cast as "pure" Christian princes or princesses, in Erasmus's terms; examples might be King Edward I in *Macbeth* or even Cordelia in

King Lear. These characters are often in the background, like a moral compass.

Instead Shakespeare finds the idealised Renaissance image of humankind scattered among a number of people. The human potential that many of his characters show combines into a future vision of a social order commensurate with the needs of humankind and so points into the future of humanity. In this respect Shakespeare's positive characters are of their time and also born before their time in terms of their potential.

In the tragedies we have found the Machiavellians to be presented as the greatest danger to the common good. They are depicted as dangerous and murderous. In each case their inhumanity causes the downfall of the tragic hero. Shakespeare's historical optimism at the beginning of the era in which we still live allows him to end his tragedies with the destruction of the Machiavellians.

Shakespeare puts all this disparate potential of his time on stage. His characters are memorable and credible, and the trajectory of their journeys remains with us and can inform the way we understand and respond to our own times.

Thinking about Hamlet, feeling his plight, we become more aware of the difference between revenge and justice—in everyday politics, where media hysteria seeking "revenge" for an atrocity will remind us of Hamlet's hesitation at pointless bloodshed. We also cherish the affirmation of human equality by the gravediggers and remember the fate of Ophelia, who was coerced into a web of deceit. Not least, Hamlet alerts us to the potential beauty of the world.

Othello is also memorable for the vision of beauty, here captured in the nature of his early relationship with Desdemona. It is an affirmation of human equality in the potential that this love had. Desdemona and Emilia remain in our minds as women of integrity, who defend reason and honesty in the face of their deaths. Further, we will always fear Iago and the power of words to distort facts and destroy dignity. This is something again that we witness daily in our own time, and *Othello* helps us see such verbal manipulation for what it is.

King Lear takes the gravediggers' understanding of human equality to a different level. His literal nakedness on the heath marks an unparalleled insight into common human nature and identification with the poorest of the poor. Lear discovers human dignity when he is stripped of everything. In today's world the plight of the refugees comes close to what Shakespeare was illustrating. Lear's recognition of human dignity, of social injustice, and the need for an equal distribution of wealth, has lost none of its urgency.

The Macbeths are different from the other tragic heroes in that they embody in one character both the potential for human kindness and its own annihilation. *Macbeth* shows us where the principle of absolute power leads. Ultimately, it destroys a person's human core and, if unapprehended, can result in the destruction of humankind. This is possibly the closest Shakespeare gets to our time. We need to think no further than our leaders' readiness for war and the destruction of the environment. For power and wealth, it seems, we are willing to countenance our own extinction.

It is Shakespeare's genius to have recognised with such clarity these conflicting potentials and driving forces of Renaissance society, which continue to this day. This is what makes his plays so important for us now.

ACKNOWLEDGEMENTS

I would like to thank most sincerely those people who helped me with their suggestions and questions while I was working on my chapters: Maureen Hirsch, Anne Brindley, Mo Ryan, Mary Murphy, Friederike Riese, Hermann Kopp, Niall Farrell, and Danny Farrell.

I would also like to thank Séamas Ó Brógáin for his conscientious proof-reading.

I am deeply indebted to Tomás Mac Síomóin for his generous support and belief in me.

Finally, I would like to remember my mother, Renate Mitchell, who spent the last year of her life in our house and who encouraged me enthusiastically in this project.

ABOUT THE AUTHOR

Jenny Farrell was born in Berlin, German Democratic Republic (GDR). She grew up in a bilingual German-Scottish-Irish family, where from an early age she was familiar with the literature and music of these traditions. She graduated from Humboldt University Berlin in 1980, with a BA and a B Ed in English and German. The same university awarded her a PhD in English Romantic Literature in 1985. She has lived in Ireland since 1985, working as a lecturer in GMIT. Her main fields of interest are Irish and English poetry and the work of William Shakespeare.

Publications:

Keats - The Progress of the Odes. Unity and Utopia, Peter Lang, 1989.
Shakespeares Tragödien–Eine Einführung, Neue Impulse Verlag, 2016.

SUGGESTED FURTHER READING

Arnold Kettle (ed.), *Shakespeare in a Changing World* (Lawrence and Wishart, 1964).

Bill Bryson, *Shakespeare: The World as a Stage* (Harper Press, 2007).

James Shapiro, *1599: A Year in the Life of William Shakespeare* (Faber and Faber, 2005).

James Shapiro, *1606: William Shakespeare and the Year of Lear* (Faber and Faber, 2015).

Kiernan Ryan, *Shakespeare* (3rd edition) (Palgrave, 2002).

Kiernan Ryan, *Shakespeare's Universality: Here's Fine Revolution* (Bloomsbury, 2015).

Robert Weimann, *Shakespeare and the Popular Tradition in the Theatre: Studies in the Social Dimension of Dramatic Form and Function* (Johns Hopkins University Press, 1978).

Robert Winder, *The Final Act of Mr Shakespeare* (Abacus, 2010)—a novel.

Made in the USA
Charleston, SC
05 September 2016